SPEND-A-LITTLE SAVE-A-LOT HOME IMPROVEMENTS

MONEY-SAVING PROJECTS ANYONE CAN DO

Brad Staggs

BETTERWAY HOME
CINCINNATI, OHIO
www.betterwaybooks.com

JUL 11

Read This Important Safety Notice

To prevent accidents, keep safety in mind while you work. Use the safety guards installed on power equipment; they are for your protection.

When working on power equipment, keep fingers away from saw blades, wear safety goggles to prevent injuries from flying wood chips and sawdust, wear hearing protection and consider installing a dust vacuum to reduce the amount of airborne sawdust in your woodshop.

Don't wear loose clothing, such as neckties or shirts with loose sleeves, or jewelry, such as rings, necklaces or bracelets, when working on power equipment. Tie back long hair to prevent it from getting caught in your equipment.

People who are sensitive to certain chemicals should check the chemical content of any product before using it.

Due to the variability of local conditions, construction materials, skill levels, etc., neither the author nor Popular Woodworking Books assumes any responsibility for any accidents, injuries, damages or other losses incurred resulting from the material presented in this book.

The authors and editors who compiled this book have tried to make the contents as accurate and correct as possible. Plans, illustrations, photographs and text have been carefully checked. All instructions, plans and projects should be carefully read, studied and understood before beginning construction.

Prices listed for supplies and equipment were current at the time of publication and are subject to change.

Metric Conversion Chart

TO CONVERT	TO	MULTIPLY BY
Inches	Centimeters	2.54
Centimeters	Inches	0.4
Feet	Centimeters	30.5
Centimeters	Feet	0.03
Yards	Meters	0.9
Meters	Yards	1.1

Distributed in Canada by Fraser Direct
100 Armstrong Avenue
Georgetown, Ontario L7G 5S4
Canada

Distributed in the U.K. and Europe by F+W Media International
Brunel House
Newton Abbot
Devon TQ12 4PU
England
Tel: (+44) 1626 323200
Fax: (+44) 1626 323319
E-mail: postmaster@davidandcharles.co.uk

Distributed in Australia by Capricorn Link
P.O. Box 704
Windsor, NSW 2756
Australia

Visit our Web site at www.popularwoodworking.com.

Other fine Popular Woodworking Books are available from your local bookstore or direct from the publisher.

14   13   12   11   10   5   4   3   2   1

ACQUISITIONS EDITOR: David Thiel
DESIGNER: Brian Roeth

About the Author

Brad Staggs is a licensed contractor and has become a regular on tlevision shows around the country and the internet. He has written, produced and directed feature stories for The Nashville Network. When HGTV launched, Brad began producing and hosting features for *Decorating with Style* and *Today at Home*, where he quickly became known as HGTVs "Home Maintenance Expert." When Scripps created DIY, Brad was brought on to host *Home Repair & Remodeling*, he also co-produced *Tools & Techniques*, and he had a role in *Decorating & Design* and *Gardening and Landscaping*. Today, Brad is seen weekly on HGTV's HGTVPro.Com Weekly. He can be seen on the syndicated *Rebecca's Garden*, *The Today Show* and recently wrapped up a stint as anchor of RFD-TV Live!, a news/information program aimed at the agricultural heartland of America.

Acknowledgements

Throughout the course of writing this book, I discovered that it takes a team to bring a project like this to life. I'm grateful to everyone on my team for the invaluable time, effort and wisdom. Ken Williams of Dickson Heating & Cooling remains one of the (seemingly) few honest & hard-working repairmen in the business. His technical know-how pulled me from the fire many times. My sister Anita Warren and friend Beth Knott were kind enough to read this book cover-to-cover. I commend you both for your keen eye and grasp of the English language; my grasp just looks tighter thanks to you. This book wouldn't have been possible had I not been my father's son. I believe it's 'Honest' Ray Staggs' DNA that gave me the ability to think outside the box in all projects I undertake. And finally, I'm grateful for my friend and editor David Thiel. Thank you for your confidence, your friendship, and mostly for your bottomless patience. You know that I have a completely new appreciation for your world.

Contents

Introduction

For most people, a home is the single most expensive investment they'll ever make, not just in terms of money but also sweat and emotional equity. With everything you've invested in your home, it makes sense to keep it and its systems running at peak efficiency, right? That's the reason this book exists.

I wanted to assemble a collection of projects that would make a real difference once completed — and not simply the same old projects normally found in a home improvement book. Each of the following pages is filled with tips and tricks I've learned through years of personal experience on job sites, as well as the many TV shows I've produced and hosted.

I truly believe that if a person has the desire to accomplish a project, and is willing to put in the time necessary to learn the techniques and tools involved, the sky is the limit. That's the goal of this book: to give you the knowledge I've gained that will manifest itself as confidence in your own abilities. Combine that newly-gained confidence with a good set of tools and you may never have to call a handyman again!

Starting Outside

From the time of the Great Flood, water has been a real source of pain and gnashing of teeth with us humans. It seems so benign, even comforting at times. Given the chance, though, water will turn on you in a heartbeat — so be prepared!

In the world of home ownership, water can lead to everything from cracked foundations to long-lasting mold problems within a structure. I've even seen the results of water pushing rocks and branches through cinder block walls. It's a pretty amazing liquid!

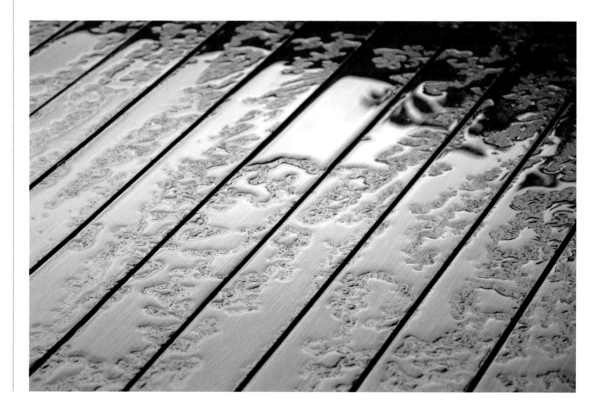

Finding a Hole in Your Roof

It's a good idea to start at the top of your house to see where water might become a problem. This, of course, means getting on the roof, since the source of most water infiltration comes from overhead — in the form of rain. You see, disguised as a gentle, refreshing rain, water cleverly diverts your attention while it looks for the smallest hole or crack in your roof. When it finds it, things can get ugly very quickly.

Roof leaks are one of the most frustrating problems in a home. Even professionals have trouble finding their source. The reason is simple — if water finds a small entryway through your roofing material, the evil force known as gravity pulls it down the underside of the sheathing for a short, or possibly long distance. It then soaks through the insulation between your ceiling joists and manifests itself inside your home as a giant ugly stain on your ceiling, or worse — in your wall where you can't even see it! That's when the mold issue can start, but we'll get to that later.

The reason it's so aggravating and tough to fix is the aforementioned gravity issue. Just because the stain appeared in your living room doesn't mean the hole is directly overhead. The good news is, there's at least one trick you can employ to find the offending hole in the roof.

LOOK FOR THE STAIN OR WORSE, THE PEELING PLASTER OR DRYWALL

Once you've discovered that you have a leak, or that your roof has one, it's time to put on your investigator's hat and take a trip into your attic. Orient yourself so that you know approximately where the stained ceiling is and head in that direction. You should do this on a rainy day, as you're more likely to catch the culprit in action.

Once you've reached the area where the water is soaking your ceiling, take a look at the roof rafters and sheathing. If the water is actively coming in, follow it up to its source. If it's not raining, look for a water stain and again, follow it to the likely point of entry. The good news is — you're about halfway to fixing the problem! Again, try to get a good idea of what section of roofing you're looking at so you can find it from the other side.

Stained roof framing is a good indicator of a roof leak.

Peeling drywall in a closet from nail pop leak!

The Short-term Solution

Generally, the problem can be a worn shingle or a sheathing nail that's worked its way loose and poked a nice hole right through the asphalt material. For a nail hole, it's best to remove the errant fastener and replace it with a galvanized screw.

1 A sheathing nail has worked its way through a shingle.

2 The short-term fix is to simply pry out the nail with a claw hammer,

3 Then drive a 2½ or 3-inch screw into the same hole.

4 Nine times out of ten, the screw will grab and hold the sheathing in place. Then, just use some roofing sealant to fill the hole in the shingle(s).

The Long-term Solution

If your roof is in otherwise good condition, it's best to simply replace the perforated shingle. It's not as complicated as it sounds and takes only a few tools: a roofing sealant, prybar, putty knife, hammer and roofing nails.

1 First, locate both ends of the damaged shingle. They should be reasonably easy to spot at a close distance. If you have dimensional shingles like these, the seams will be a little more difficult to find (if the roofers did their job correctly), so spend a little time looking.

2 Once you've spotted the elusive edges, use the putty knife to gently release the seal along the leading edge of the shingle. You'll also most likely have to repeat this process on the shingle above, as the nails securing it will be holding the one you're trying to remove.

3 You should be able to see 3 or 4 nails holding the shingle in place.

4 Hint: A small block of wood works well for holding the shingle in place while you work.

5 Use the prybar to remove the nails.

6 You may have to use the hammer for leverage. Once you've removed the nails from the damaged shingle, you're still not done! Depending on the nailing pattern used, the shingle(s) in the row just above may also need removal. Isn't this fun? Take it slowly, you'll be able to tell if it's difficult to pry the shingle loose. Patience is key when working on a roof.

7 (ABOVE LEFT) If necessary, remove the nails from the shingles just above the one you're replacing. Congratulations, it's time to remove the old shingle and replace it. It'll give you a great sense of accomplishment.

8 (ABOVE RIGHT) Try to find a shingle that matches not only the color of the one you're replacing, but also the shingle pattern.

9 (LEFT) After you've removed the shingle, check for any obvious damage to the shingles, roofing paper and sheathing underneath. You don't need to fill the nail holes from the shingle you just removed, but make sure there aren't any holes the size of small animals. Those you'll need to fix!

10 Insert the new shingle in place and secure with four nails in the locations indicated on the illustration at right.

Shingle Nailing Pattern

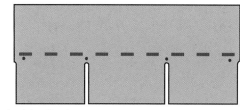

Standard Applications

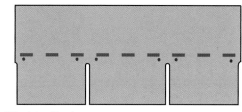

High Wind Applications

11 The new shingle has a sealant strip that should self-seal over the course of a few warm days, but I like to apply a thin bead of asphalt sealant along its edge, as well as the leading edges of any shingles I've had to pry up during the job.

⊕ BRAD'S TIP

If you look around and see this problem repeated several times over the entire roof area, you may want to consider installing new shingles. Yes, this gets expensive quickly, but the money you save by preventing significant water leakage in the future may well be worth it.

Checking & Repairing Flashing

The word "flashing" has a myriad of meanings. In this case, we're talking about thin sheets of metal that are used to keep water from infiltrating your home. They're generally used around chimneys, where two different roof lines meet, and around skylights, to name but a couple of the possible applications.

These are the areas we'll focus on in this section, since they are the most likely to cause a lot of damage if they fail. Because they're all on the roof, if they don't do their job, you have the potential for having a waterfall in your living room, bedroom or den.

Closely following roofing nail pops, flashing failures are the most likely places that you'll find leaks in your home's structure. Keeping flashing locations clean and sealed is the best defense against a large repair bill.

First, a word from our legal department team. Remember safety any time you're working on a roof! Wear slip-resistant shoes, always secure your ladder so it stays put and tether yourself whenever possible!

Chimney Flashing

Let's again start at the top...of the roof. In this case, that's where the chimney sits and it's often the source of water infiltration.

The flashing around your chimney should be free of major gaps and cracks. It should be well adhered to the roofing material and nails should be covered with roofing cement. That would be a perfect world, wouldn't it?

Unfortunately, you'll find a lot of flashing in this condition (shown right and below) around a chimney.

It's not so much the rust that bothers me here, but the gaps where the metal meets the asphalt, so to speak. Areas like these can lead to rain finding its way to places it shouldn't be — like inside your home.

The first step to fixing the situation is getting the debris and old sealant out of the way. While this flashing needs the repair all along its lower edge, we'll just work a section of it to give you an idea of how to fix it. Sometimes it's easier to work small areas to keep from getting overwhelmed, especially on a roof.

We'll be working with some basic tools on this project. You'll need a claw hammer, a putty knife, gloves (flashing can have very sharp edges), galvanized roofing nails (the ones I'm working with have small rubber washers on them that help seal the area around the nail, but the washers are NOT mandatory!), rubberized roofing/flashing repair in a caulk tube and, of course, a caulk gun.

1 The first step is to remove the old sealant from the flashing where it meets the roofing material. Use the putty knife to gently (without damaging the shingles) remove the old, hardened lumps. Be aware that there are probably some nails hiding in the old sealant. In this case, they were so loose they could be removed by hand! If they're still holding tight, leave them in place!

One of the reasons the old nails didn't hold is they were too short! The nails we'll use to resecure the flashing are about an inch and a quarter long, so they penetrate the shingles and end up in the roof sheathing.

2 If the flashing is loose enough to expose the shingles underneath, you'll need to remove the dried sealant under the leading edge, as well. Again, use the putty knife to remove the debris. If it's still adhered well, though, it's best not to disturb it.

3 Once you have the area cleaned up, cut the tip of the caulk tube at roughly a 45 degree angle, leaving a ¼"-hole exposed. Then insert the tube into the caulk gun.

4 Next, lay a medium-sized bead of caulk under the leading edge of the flashing. Use the handle of the putty knife to hold the flashing up and out of the way if necessary.

5 Once the sealant is in place, remove the putty knife and reposition so that you can fill that area with sealant as well. Then, press the flashing firmly into place to make sure the sealant makes contact all along the edge. It should ooze out slightly.

6 Then, place a nail in the existing nail hole or adjacent to it if the existing hole has been expanded. Drive it flush to the surface of the flashing with the hammer. Be careful not to overdrive the nail as this could bend the flashing out of shape and cause it to bow upward...not a good thing! Once the nail is holding the flashing securely in place, it's time to seal the top of it. Run a bead of sealant along the top of the leading edge, covering the nail head. Use the putty knife to spread the bead evenly across the top of the leading edge. Avoid leaving a hump that could act as a dam for water. You want any moisture to flow as smoothly as possible over the flashing and down the roof.

◆ BRAD'S TIP

If the flashing tends to bend upward at the corner, try bending it in the opposite direction so that it lies as flat as possible on the roof. Apply the sealant as directed above and then use the hammer as a wedge to hold it in place until the sealant sets. Once the sealant cures, it should hold the flashing securely in place. If necessary, add another nail at the corner, but do so only as a last resort. Remember, the fewer nail holes in a roof, the fewer chances for water to get in!

7 Next, take a look at the corners of the chimney where the flashing is secured. This is another area where water tends to find a way into your home. If there are gaps, use the sealant to seal them and the putty knife to smooth them out.

8 Finally, look along the face and sides of the chimney where the flashing terminates at the brick. If you see cracks or gaps in this area, seal them up, as well. If your chimney is painted, as this one is, use a paintable masonry caulk like the one described in the "Filling Cracks in Concrete" section of this book. Fill the gaps or cracks with the caulk and feather it into the surrounding area. If you're feeling truly ambitious, you can remove the old sealant, but I'm all about getting the job done and getting out...and if the old sealant is stuck pretty well, I wouldn't mess with it.

An easy way to see if your sealing job is effective is to take a look inside your attic where the chimney meets the roof. Do this on a rainy day and look for any damp spots. Hopefully, you won't see any, but if you do... you'll know right where to look back on the roof!

Skylight Flashing

Generally, what's referred to as "step-flashing" is used around the perimeter of skylights. It could be any number of short (up to about 12 inches long) pieces of aluminum that overlap each other down each side of the window.

These are tied into longer lengths of flashing along the top and bottom that work together to keep water from seeping in around the perimeter.

I've removed the skylight from its position so that you can better see the step-flashing. I don't advise you do the same. Just take a peek under the rim of the glass frame.

The most important thing you can do in this situation is to keep dirt and debris from building up around the edges. This organic material can cause miniature dams that allow water to flow back up and under the flashing and shingles.

Simply use a whisk broom or brush to sweep away the debris in the fall. Generally, a couple of cleanings a year is sufficient for this job, but if you have large trees that shed limbs or twigs, you might have to do it more often.

If you notice any nails protruding from the flashing, drive them back in (as described in the chimney flashing repair), coating the head of the nail with flashing sealant.

Roof Flashing

Check the areas where any two different roof lines meet on your home. You should see metal flashing similar to this.

Check for any rips or tears in the surface of the flashing. Use a small amount of clear silicone sealant to patch the hole if necessary.

This type of flashing tends to hold up pretty well, since it's on a vertical surface and generally shielded. In some cases an object like a tree limb has made contact making a tear. Also look closely at any seams that may have become separated.

There could be a sealant of some form holding a seam like this together. If any foreign objects have become lodged in the seam, simply remove them. To prevent damaging the flashing, use a foam paint roller to flatten out any seams that may have become bent over time.

By taking a little time each year to inspect the flashing on your roof, you could be saving literally thousands of dollars in repairs. Remember the mantra, "Water will find a way!" It's your job to keep the roadblocks in place and performing their best!

In the Gutter

The gutters on your home are designed to collect and disperse the water that runs off your roof. Without the gutters, rainwater simply falls directly off the eaves and ends up way too close to your house's foundation. This can lead to serious problems, like flooded basements and crawl spaces, cracked concrete or cinderblock foundation walls. And don't forget that nasty, moldy, mildewy smell that gets embarrassing when company comes over!

Keeping your gutters and downspouts in good shape is a wise investment, both financially and in terms of your hard-earned spare time. In most cases, you should be able to get your system in tip-top shape for less than a couple hundred bucks. That pales in comparison to foundation repair — or replacement, as I once had to do. That bill was a measly $46,000. I'll let you do the math.

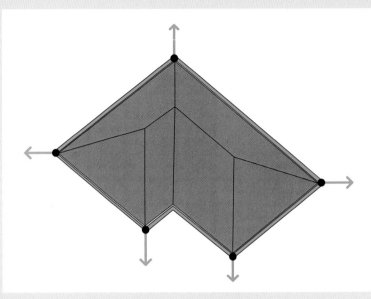

Gutters and downspouts (the black dots) collect water from the roof and disperse it away from your home's foundation

Pieces and Parts

The gutters themselves will either be of the seamless variety (generally installed by professionals) or installed as sections (anywhere from 10 to 16 ft. in length). Both types use some type of fastening system to keep them in place. The most common is the gutter spike.

Over time, these spikes tend to work themselves loose from the fascia board that they're fastened to (left). This is most likely because they split the wood when they were installed and weren't sealed properly to prevent moisture from seeping into the fascia and swelling the wood. As we say in the South, the holes got wallered out.

The result of gutter spikes pulling loose from fascia board.

The best fix for this problem is called a gutter screw. It's like a spike, but better — instead of being pounded in like a nail, it screws in using a drill/driver. In most cases, gutter screws are designed to be used in the same holes that the spikes came loose from, making the swap pretty simple. Just remember to use the sleeve provided with the new screw or the one that came off the old spike, if it fits. This prevents you from over-driving the screw and crushing your gutter...leading to another repair expense!

This one simple fix can save literally thousands of dollars in repairs due to gutter failure and the resulting water damage to your eaves and foundation!

(MIDDLE RIGHT) A gutter screw with included sleeve. (RIGHT) Install gutter screws with a drill/driver and be sure to use the sleeve to avoid damaging the gutter!

Clear leaves and other organic debris from the gutter before continuing to the next step. A garden hose is the best tool for the job.

Sealing the Joints

If your gutters were installed in sections, chances are that one or more of the joints connecting each section (Photo 1) are leaking. The good news? It's a pretty simple fix. All you need to do is wait for a dry day, then thoroughly clean the area on the inside of the gutter on both sides of the joint.

Start with a soapy water solution (Photo 2) and finish the job with some mineral spirits (Photo 3) to get any old sealant off the surface. Allow it to dry completely, then apply some silicone sealant along the inside of the joint. Smooth it out using a wood shim or putty knife (Photo 4). This will prevent the sealant from becoming a "speed bump."

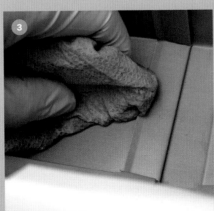

Topping It Off

Once your gutters are securely in place, it's time to make sure that the only thing that gets into them is water. Anything else that finds its way into the gutters either ends up weighing it down (remember those pesky gutter spikes that pulled out?) or simply clogging it and the downspouts.

The easiest and most effective way to make sure that water is the only thing in your gutter is by installing some sort of lid, topper or gutter guard. They come in several different shapes and a couple of sizes.

Gutter guards come in a variety of styles and are generally made from plastic or aluminum. Starting from the left: plastic mesh without screen; plastic mesh with built-in screen; wire mesh with clips. A solid plastic guard is shown in place on the gutter.

WIRE MESH

The first type of gutter guard is of the wire-mesh variety, which has the advantage of being probably the least expensive and is easy to install. This particular style attaches to the gutter's outer lip with small clips that double as hinges. Once attached, you simply fold the guard back and lay it across the top of the shingles.

It works reasonably well, but isn't my favorite because it tends to catch leaf stems and pine needles in the tiny holes. That leaves you (pun intended) back where you started, with organic material causing a problem with water flow into the gutter.

PLASTIC MESH

Second in line is the plastic-mesh style. It installs by sliding over the entire front lip of your home's gutters. The challenge can be getting it to fit snugly over areas where the gutter may be bent. It is less prone to bending than the wire-mesh and has the added advantage of possibly matching your gutter's color — as long as it's white, off-white or brown (in most cases).

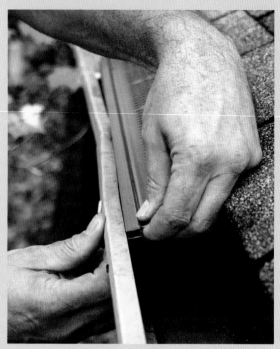

This plastic-mesh style has a lower profile and tends to be more "invisible" than other styles.

SOLID PLASTIC

Last, and holding the distinction of being my favorite method of gutter protection, are the solid plastic sections that use friction to direct water into the gutter. These allow leaves and other debris to roll off the leading edge and fall to the ground, where you're forced to rake them up or mow them into mulch, which in turn fertilizes your lawn!

"Solid" plastic guards also snap along the front edge of the gutters and slide underneath the first layer of shingles.

Dispersing the Water

Every gutter system should have several downspouts. Their job is to carry the water collected by the gutter and channel it away from the foundation of the house. Sounds simple enough, but problems can arise quickly when they become clogged or simply drain too close to the exterior wall.

The first problem is often alleviated when gutter toppers are installed, but before that time, leaves and debris collected by the gutter can cause a virtual logjam at the downspout's entry point inside the gutter. For this reason, it's important to clear any debris from the gutter before it gets to that point.

If the gutter gunk finds its way into the downspout, it can cause a clog you can't even see. This can force water out through unsealed joints or worse, back into the gutter itself, adding to that weight issue we discussed earlier. See how this is all connected?

So, let's stop the problem before it starts.

All you need is a garden hose to clear most clogs from a downspout. Just insert it at the top and turn it on. The water pressure should dislodge any stubborn debris from inside, which will then come rushing out the bottom; this is a good reason to stand back a bit to avoid getting any of that smelly decomposing stuff on you.

Once the downspouts are cleared, take a look at where they empty out. Traditional wisdom says they should send the water anywhere from 2 to 4 feet away from your home's foundation. That's a pretty good rule of thumb.

Splash blocks are a good way to ensure that the water heads off into the yard and not back up against the house. They should be installed so that the open end is toward your yard. Otherwise, water can roll back up the sloped form and back up against your house. You know how that story can end.

One reason some people turn their splash blocks around is because they can cause some erosion to occur as water rushes down and into the soil, particularly during heavy rains. A better solution to this problem is using an inexpensive device (around $10) called a downspout drain. You simply attach it to to the end of the downspout with the included bracket.

During dry periods, the disperser stays neatly coiled and out of the way.

When it rains, though, it uncoils and disperses the water over a wider area, with less chance of erosion. It can actually be a source of entertainment if you get really bored.

⊕ BRAD'S TIP

To move water even farther into your yard, simply install a short section of downspout (anywhere from two to four feet in length), to the end of your existing downspout, then add the downspout drain. I used this method to carry water out past a client's shrubs and into her yard, where it drained harmlessly away from her already cracked foundation.

Sloping the Earth

This step requires a little heavy lifting, as you can imagine. Actually, we're just talking about sloping the earth (small "e") around your home's foundation so that any water that happens to hit it will have a tendency to roll away from your house as opposed to slamming into the exterior wall.

Remember I said that water will find a way? It's true. Water that lands next to the foundation can soak down through the soil, under the con-crete slab or through the foundation wall, and cause a whole lot of damage. That's why you need to check all areas around your home and particularly around downspouts and flower beds.

Be sure the dirt is sloped at least ⅛ inch for every linear foot it travels from the house. If you have to buy dirt to fill in low spots, just do an online search for "fill dirt" in your area or check with a landscaper or contractor nearby and ask them where to find the best deal.

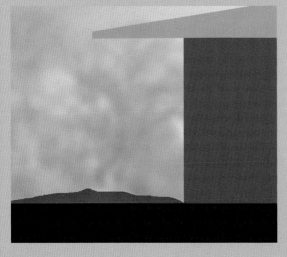

Improperly Sloped Land

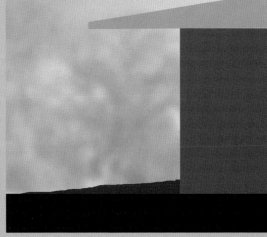

Properly Sloped Land

HVAC–Heating & Air Conditioning

HVAC stands for heating, ventilation, and air conditioning. In general terms, it's the largest appliance system you most likely have in your home. It might even be the most expensive piece of equipment you own, with the possible exception of some high-end stoves and refrigerators. This is a fact that many people learn only when their system needs replacing and they begin getting estimates.

CHAPTER 2

The Basics

If you think about it, you probably spend some time cleaning your oven (or at least setting it to clean itself) and vacuuming the coils on your refrigerator (if you don't, you should as it can prevent premature failure of that appliance!). It makes sense, then, that you spend a little time each month making sure your HVAC system is clean, tight and bright, as my high school auto shop teacher used to say about cars. He was a wise man and if heeded, his words could save you a lot of money and trouble in the long run.

The most common type of HVAC system in use is the split system. It is composed of an inside unit that con-tains a furnace, an evaporator and an air-handling unit, and an outside unit that houses a condenser and com-pressor. Both units share a need to be clean to operate at their peak efficiency.

KEEP IT CLUTTER-FREE

Both the inside and outside units of a split system need their breathing room. Inside, a gas furnace needs good airflow for proper operation. It's also a good idea to keep anything combustible away from the unit.

The inside portion of a standard HVAC system is shown above. Notice the clutter around the unit on the left. It's best to keep the area around the unit as clean and clutter-free as possible. This unit is in a basement. HVAC systems can also be located in an attic or crawl space.

With the space around this equipment clear of obstructions, it has better airflow and can operate more efficiently when the furnace is running.

The outside compressor needs airflow as well to run at top efficiency. Keep the area around the unit clear of unnecessary clutter and debris. Do not store gas cans or other combustible materials near it.

We'll cover more on how to make sure this unit is working properly later, but simply keeping the area clean around it is a good start!

The picture at right shows a compressor with too much clutter around it. It's especially unwise to store things like gasoline around this unit!

Sweep away any dirt and debris from around the compressor unit.

The area is clean and clear of obstructions, as it should be.

Checking & Replacing Filters

Inside your home, the single most important thing you can do to ensure the long life and health of your furnace and air handler is change the filters on a monthly basis. It sounds so simple, and yet it is the one thing that comes up again and again when I talk to friends in the HVAC business. If people would simply change their filters monthly and have their systems serviced once a year, the world would be a happier place. OK, well maybe just inside your home — but that's a start!

The process is simple. The air intakes (the number you have depends on the size and number of systems your home has) pull air from inside your home and send it through the air handler once it's been heated or cooled. Because so much air is passed through these intakes over the course of each day, the crud that builds on their surface is pretty incredible — and sometimes disgusting.

Above left is a look at an air filter that was in place for about two months in a 3500 square foot home. It's one of three filters in the home. The clear area in the middle is where a small piece of the plastic cello packaging got stuck when it was installed. It shows

you how much crud, dirt, dander and dust are caught before they can enter the mechanics of your system! At right is another of the filters on the same system.

The photo at left shows a new filter on the left sitting next to a two-month-old filter on the right. Notice that there is NO light coming through the dirty filter. This homeowner waited too long to change the filter and probably paid for it in higher utility bills!

Think of the system like your car. When your car's air filter gets clogged with debris like this, your car starts to run poorly, getting bad gas mileage. You notice it when you go to fill up and see that you're not getting the miles per gallon that you're used to.

In your home, you may notice that rooms are getting too hot or too cold or that there is a minimal amount of air coming out of the vents. These are signs that the system is having a hard time breathing! Time to change the filter!

First, turn the system to the "Off" position.

Locate the return air grills on your system. Remember, there could be more than 1, and all filters should be changed at the same time.

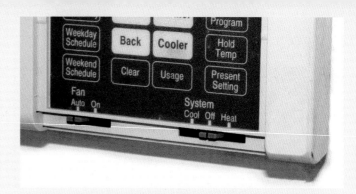

Most modern system thermostats have an "Off" position. If yours does not, simply turn the thermostat to a setting that will prevent the unit from coming on during the procedure. In other words, turn the system to "Heat" and lower the temperature to the lowest setting.

Both of these return ducts are located in the same home and the filters should be changed at the same time to ensure system efficiency!

The intake grates will have either small levers or screws that allow them to hinge down, exposing the filter. Sometimes these tiny levers get a little tough to open. You can use a screwdriver or even a coin to pry them up if you can't get them released with your fingers.

Once you open the grill, carefully pry out the old, dirty filter, being careful not to shake off too much of the debris stuck to it.

Install the new filter, making sure the airflow arrows are pointing inward.

It's a good idea to mark the filter with the date you changed it. That way, there's no doubt when it should be changed again!

Notice that the filter above became so clogged that the system almost pulled it into the duct! This type of distortion of the filter means that the owner waited too long to change it out for a new one!

Finally, before closing the grill, use a vacuum to clean up around the entire intake area. This will keep the dust, dirt and hair that's accumulated from ending up in the filter in the next 10 minutes!

Just like the equipment itself, the return air grates must be kept free of clutter and debris — or, furniture, as it were. Putting tables or chairs in front of them can inhibit airflow and cause your system to waste energy.

Fixing Hot & Cold Spots

Every house has them — or at least every house I've ever been in, anyway. They are hot and cold spots and they're annoying at best.

You may have a bedroom that stays too hot in the summer and too cold in the winter. Or maybe some other room in your home just seems uncooperative when it comes to air conditioning. The good news is the problem is most likely a simple fix.

Let's start with the most obvious — the supply-air grill. If it has adjustable louvers, they may simply be closed too much. If a room is uncomfortable during any time of the year when the system's running, this could be the problem.

Simply opening the louvers on a vent grill can make a room more comfortable, especially if the louvers have been in the closed position. Closing off vents also puts stress on the rest of the system and can damage the air-handling unit. A vent should never be completely closed for that reason.

If adjusting the vent louvers doesn't fix the issue, try tracing the duct back to the main air-handling unit. It may run in the attic or the basement. Once you find it, there's a good chance that it has an air damper lever somewhere along its run.

The air damper acts like a stopper inside the duct itself — allowing more or less air to flow through the duct and to the vents in each room. It's possible that the damper is restricting airflow to such a degree that it's causing some rooms to be uncomfortable.

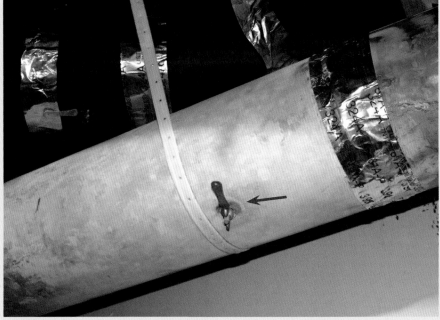

The lever on the duct is oriented in-line with the damper disc inside. In this photo, you can see that the damper is nearly closed.

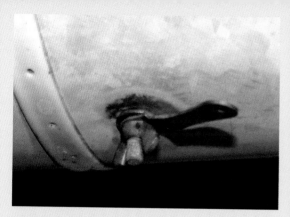

By moving the lever slightly, airflow through the duct is increased and may cure the imbalanced system. Care should be taken to move the lever in small incremental amounts. For instance, if you think about it in terms of a clock, the lever above is slightly past the two o'clock position. By moving it only to the four o'clock position, the problem may be cured. To change the damper's position, loosen the wing nut, turn the lever slightly, then tighten the nut to prevent the damper from moving around.

Another view of a duct damper lever. If the lever is hard to move, try loosening the wing nut on the pivot post. Be sure to retighten after adjustment.

Adjusting the dampers on your system can be tricky. It can cause reduced air pressure to the rest of your home and may cause heating and cooling issues in other rooms. For this reason, be sure you make only minor adjustments! If there is no result or if it causes problems in other areas of your home, the damper may not be the issue!

While not as likely, another area to check is the connection of the ducts to the main trunk of the line. I've seen ducting that's come completely loose from the main due to recent maintenance in a home. It might have just slipped slightly due to air pressure or being bumped or jarred.

Obviously this duct won't be doing the inside of the house any favors! Care should be taken when fitting the two ends together, as the edges of metal ducting can be very sharp!

Locating a Leak

Far more likely than the obvious disconnected duct is a loose connection or damaged duct. Over the years, especially in older homes, the tape used to connect metal duct can fail. It may be a metal tape or a white or gray material used to secure the joint.

The simplest cure for this type of leak is to wrap the joint with a modern duct-sealing tape. Use at least two or three wraps and check for any air leaking from the duct after the repair.

When dealing with flexible duct, the same rule applies. If you find a leaky joint or a tear in the jacket around the duct, use repair tape to seal up the leak. In the case of small tears, it's not necessary to wrap the tape completely around the duct; just be sure to seal the hole with an adequately sized patch.

If, after checking the entire system and making the adjustments and/or repairs above, your system still isn't performing as you think it should, there's still hope! It may need a good cleaning and refrigerant charge. While I recommend you leave the charging to the pros, you can certainly do some of the cleaning yourself.

⊕ SAFETY FIRST! ⊕

In some older homes, a sealing tape containing asbestos was used to seal joints in HVAC systems. Use caution if you suspect this to be the case in your home. While the tape poses little danger according to many reports, you may wish to have a professional inspect your system and advise you of the best course of action.

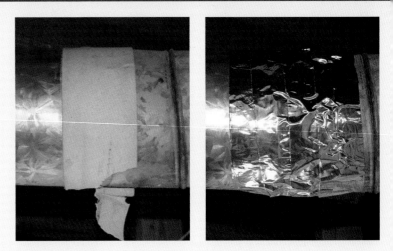

This joint started leaking because the tape originally used to seal it had failed. Several wraps of a modern sealing tape was all it took to stop the energy-wasting leak!

Flexible duct can be damaged in a number of ways. Even if the damage does not penetrate through to the air-carrying core, it's a good idea to seal up areas like this to prevent further damage from occurring.

Use enough tape to adequately cover the damaged area and use moderate pressure to make sure it sticks. If the area to be patched is dusty or dirty, clean it with a damp sponge or rag before applying the patch.

POWERED VENT

If all else fails, you can try using a powered vent. It works with a built-in thermostat to pull more air into the room you're trying to adjust. It simply replaces the existing grill and plugs into the wall. These are available for around $60.

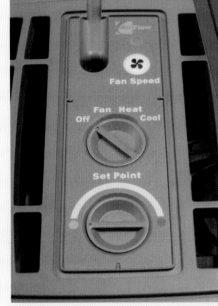

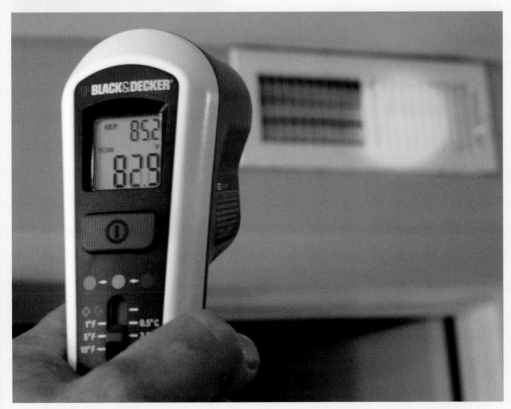

SYSTEM CHECK TOOL

Thermal leak detectors like this one can be used to find energy leaks around your home. They're also good for checking the temperature of the air coming from your HVAC system. They can alert you to a potential problem!

Cleaning the Condenser Unit

Generally, this service is included in an annual inspection/tune-up package from a pro, but I like to give my outside unit a good cleaning before shutting it down for the winter.

Some HVAC systems have only one outside condenser unit, while some homes have multiple systems servicing different areas of the house. It's important to know which system you're dealing with before making adjustments or repairs and cleaning. If you're not sure, a local HVAC service pro can help you in identifying each unit.

A close inspection of the metal fins around the condenser unit can tell you whether it needs to be cleaned. Remember, it needs good airflow to work properly and if the fins are clogged or bent, the restricted airflow could cause your system to work with less than stellar results!

The first thing to do is make sure the system thermostat is turned to the "Off" position.

The main power going to the unit must also be turned off. In most cases, there is a breaker near the unit. You may have to pull the fuses out or turn the switch "Off".

Condensing units shapes and sizes. You can also look up information online about your specific model.

When working around breakers (especially 220 volt breakers), it's a good idea to tape off the breaker while you're working with the unit. While you may be the only one at home, the tape serves as a good reminder for yourself, as well.

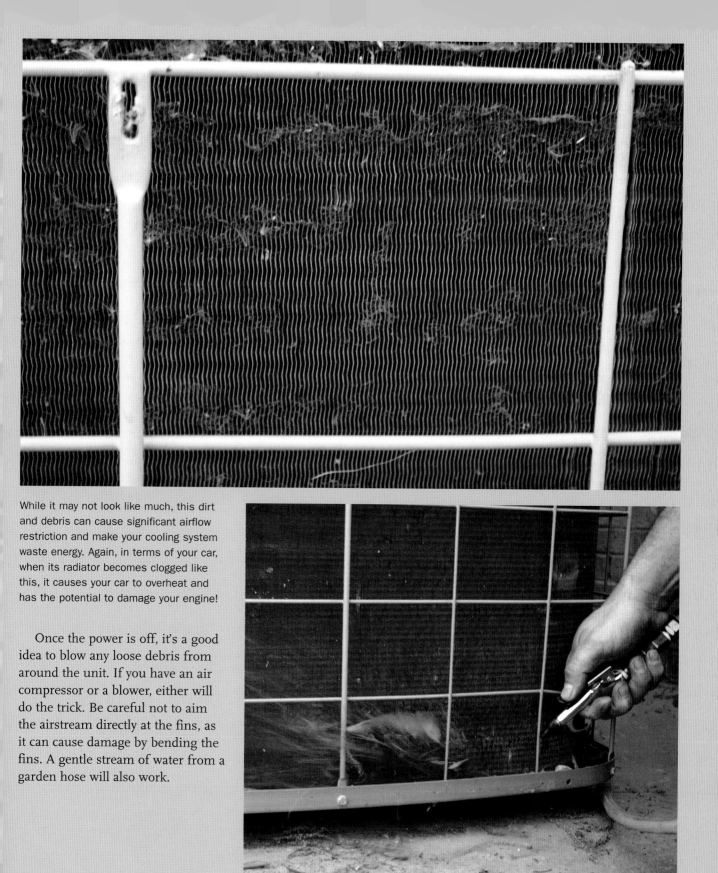

While it may not look like much, this dirt and debris can cause significant airflow restriction and make your cooling system waste energy. Again, in terms of your car, when its radiator becomes clogged like this, it causes your car to overheat and has the potential to damage your engine!

Once the power is off, it's a good idea to blow any loose debris from around the unit. If you have an air compressor or a blower, either will do the trick. Be careful not to aim the airstream directly at the fins, as it can cause damage by bending the fins. A gentle stream of water from a garden hose will also work.

Once all the loose crud is removed, it's time to take a look inside. The top of the compressor is usually held in place with several screws. Be sure to familiarize yourself with the locations of the screws that hold the top on and don't remove any other fasteners.

You should also note that the fan is connected directly to the top of the unit and can make it very heavy. You may need help removing it.

If the wiring between the unit and top is short, find a way to secure the top so that you can access the inside of the unit. You may have to lean it against a nearby wall or have someone hold it while you clean. Again, use extreme caution and care during this process to avoid damaging the equipment or hurting yourself!

Use a vacuum to remove leaves and other debris from inside the unit.

In the photo above, the top has been removed and set to the side. Be careful that it doesn't lean against the fins of the unit! Also, be careful not to bend or damage the fan blades, as this could cause them to become unbalanced.

Once cleared of debris, use a garden hose (set to shower or flat) to wet down the fins on the coil. Just like air pressure can damage the fins, so can excess water pressure, so be sure to be gentle but firm on this step.

The idea behind this step is to loosen up the crud and grime so the cleaner can do its job. I like to spray from the inside out to avoid pressing debris farther into the coil fins.

There are several brands of cleaners available to clean the the coils. You can usually find them in the HVAC area of the hardware or home improvement store for under $10 a can.

Be sure to follow all label instructions and use all necessary safety gear, including goggles to avoid getting any product into your eyes!

According to the manufacturer's instructions, spray the cleaner onto the outside of the coil fins and allow it to cut through the grime.

Once the cleaner has had a chance to work, use the hose, again spraying from the inside out, until the water runs clear through the coil.

When the debris is cleared from the fins, the water should run through the coil to the outside, forcing any remaining material with it.

Once clean, you should be able to see light through the unit. This will ensure optimum airflow.

Replace the top, reinstall the fasteners and turn the breaker to the unit back to the "On" position. Then restart the thermostat and see if your system does a better job cooling your home.

Fin Damage

As noted earlier, it's important to avoid bending the fins on the system. This blocks air from flowing across the coil and causes heat buildup. If you accidentally damage the fins or if your unit has been dented in the past, there are a couple of ways to fix the problem, using extreme care!

First, a small screwdriver can be used to gently straighten the fins, but can be very time consuming and tedious.

There are also specialty tools called "fin combs" designed to do the job. They are readily available online or in some auto-parts stores.

Before you purchase one, measure the number of fins per linear inch on your compressor and buy a comb that has that number of fins. Take your time during the straightening process to avoid further damage!

Also be aware that it takes some finesse to use a tool like this. Don't get frustrated if you don't get perfect results right away!

A fin comb can straighten most dents in the condenser unit. Use caution and take your time during the process. These combs run anywhere from less than $10 to more than $20.

Winterizing the Condenser Unit

Once you know you won't be using your air conditioner for the season, it's a good idea to cover it up. You can sometimes find custom covers at hardware stores, but the simplest way to do it is with a tarp.

Wrap the unit so that the folds of the tarp won't collect rainwater and secure it with bungee cords or clips. Be sure to uncover it before the first use the following season! A good way to prevent accidental damage is by removing the breaker or disconnect from the panel next to the unit and placing it under the tarp.

A cover will prevent a season's worth of leaves and debris from collecting inside the unit while it sits unused.

Easy Ways to Save Energy

Before you go running through your house with a caulk gun ready to seal every crack and crevice in sight, let's spend a moment thinking about where and why leaks occur. And when I say leaks, I mean air leaks. These are the small openings that are present in every home in the country that allow the inside air to leak out and the outside air to leak in causing drafts and lost money in the form of higher energy bills.

CHAPTER 3

The Logic Behind Leaks

When a home is built, it generally consists of a lot of wood nailed together, some insulation and drywall added, then small strips of wood trim slapped up to cover all the little cracks and holes you'd see otherwise. In most cases, the builder will take the time to fill the small voids around window and doorframes that could potentially be sources of air penetration. If you have an older home, chances are that the builder simply used wads of fiberglass insulation stuffed into those gaps to do the job. Or the builder may have used nothing at all!

In these photos of a door in a house I'm renovating, you can see the gap the trim was covering. In this case, the builder simply left an empty void, creating an area where air can leak. It may not seem like much, but if you add up all of the small nooks and crannies like this one, you'll end up with a hole the size of a window. And since you most likely wouldn't leave a window open and the furnace or air conditioner running, doesn't it make sense to close these holes as well?

If you've ever taken off the trim from around a window or door and noticed that the insulation used to fill the small voids in the framing has turned black, you'll understand why using insulation is a great way to simply filter the air. The insulation turned dark because of the dust and dirt particles that were caught as the air passed back and forth. Unfortunately, fiberglass insulation does little to stop the movement of the air.

That's why in modern homes, spray foam is often used to fill the voids. It creates a solid barrier that cuts down tremendously on the amount of air that can leak in — or out. You can see in this photo that the gap between the door frame and the wall framing was filled to do just that.

That being said, it would be not only messy but time-consuming and costly to rip all the trim boards from around your windows and doors to install spray foam. Instead, we'll use caulk to create a secondary barrier to air leakage. It's more convenient and economical, and will do a great job at saving you the energy dollars.

While we're at it, it's a good idea to check these areas for gaps and openings:
- Dryer vents
- Cable and electrical line openings in exterior walls
- Around water spigots outside
- Light fixtures inside and out

Each of these areas is a candidate for either caulk, spray foam insulation, or in the case of a light fixture, a good drywall repair job, at the very least. All of these areas with small openings have the potential to let air pass through, and can lead to serious energy dollars lost!

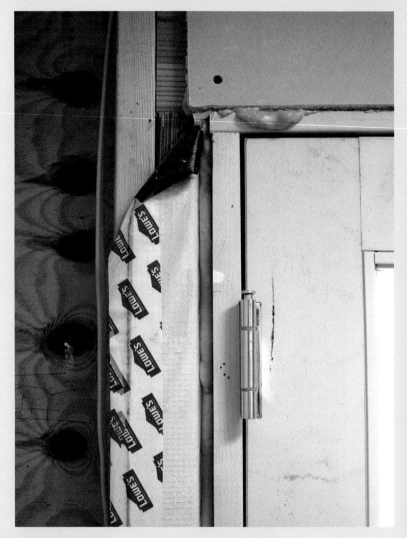

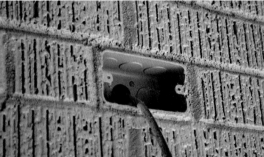

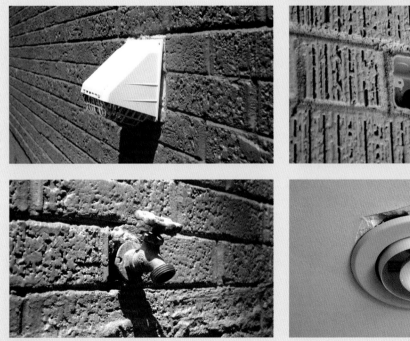

Knowing whether or not gaps are sealed is a relatively simple process. You can hold a lit match near window frames and doorframes and see if the flame flickers. If so, the window or door is a likely candidate for a sealing job.

Just a reminder, make sure you never leave a lit match unattended and use caution when dealing with fire.

A candle or stick of incense is another way to detect leaks and less likely to burn your fingers! Don't leave them burning unattended either!

There are also devices called thermal leak detectors on the market. They used to be only in the hands of professionals, but are now becoming a common item in home toolboxes. They usually cost less than $50 and are just plain fun to use.

Thermal Leak
Detector

You begin by aiming the sensor at a wall in your home to get a "base" reading. Then simply aim it at everything else, from door frames to baseboard, to see if there is a significant temperature difference. If so, you probably have an air leak and a starting point for your sealing project.

With this particular tool, you can adjust the settings to detect specific temperature variations. If an object or area is hotter or colder than your base reading, it will be signified by a red or blue light.

Tools like this one make the process of fine-tuning your home a little more fun, but don't feel like you have to run out and buy one. The candles, matches and incense are cheap and probably already in your kitchen drawer.

With that said, let's take on one of the simplest projects in an older home — weather-stripping old, leaky windows.

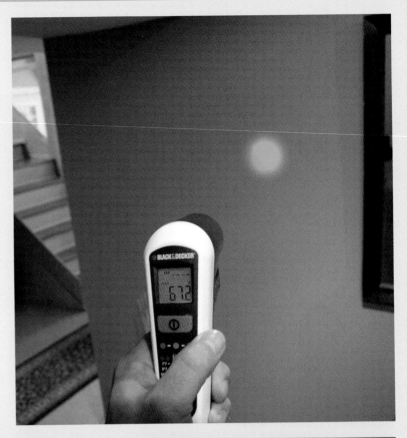

Weatherstripping Drafty Windows

There are two types of old windows in this world: those that have been painted shut for years, and those that are drafty and hard to open and close. If you have an older home, you know what I mean. We have learned at least one thing from those old windows, though — paint makes a great sealant! If you have the drafty style, there's a pretty simple fix that can cut down dramatically the amount of air that can escape or enter through the window.

Weatherstripping comes in several varieties. The most common type used for sealing gaps and cracks around windows is called "closed-cell foam". It's flexible, and has an adhesive backing that will stick to just about anything! Sold in small rolls, it's inexpensive and easy to use.

1 Once you've identified your leaky window, open it up about halfway. Measure the bottom edge of the window from side to side. Be sure to measure all the way to the window frame on each side. And remember… measure twice and cut once!

2 Once you have your measurement, use scissors to cut a length of the weatherstripping. Don't remove the backing at this time, though.

3 Clean the bottom edge of the window frame with a damp towel. Be sure to remove any remnants of old weatherstripping that may be present. The surface needs to be clean and smooth for the new seal to do its job.

4 Once the area has dried completely, start at one end of the window and slowly peel a small section of the backing off the weatherstripping material. Press the strip in place.

5 Slowly make your way across the bottom of the frame, removing only about 6 to 8 inches of backing at a time. Also, be careful not to stretch the foam or it will lose some of its ability to seal the gap!

6 Continue along the entire length of the window, being sure to smooth out any lumps or bumps.

7 Just as an insurance policy, I like to run a second strip of foam on the leading edge of the frame. This gives me two lines of protection against air leakage. Apply the second strip in the same manner as the first.

8 To give yourself a sense of accomplishment (and to see how well you did the job), you can test the area again for leaks using your favorite method. If you still see signs of air movement, make sure the weatherstripping material has adhered correctly.

Weather-sealing Windows & Doors

Once windows and doors are properly weatherstripped, take a look at the trim molding. Remember, this stuff is used to hide gaps and cracks, not seal them! And if the builder didn't do it, it's up to you to make sure you're not letting your store-bought air (as my dad says) outside!

Inspect the area where the trim meets the wall and where it's fastened to the frame of the door or window. Generally speaking, the area between the trim and window frame or doorframe is likely sealed after years of being painted, but along the wall could be a different story!

Even small cracks like the one above can allow enough air movement to cause energy loss. Spaces like the one shown at right really need to be filled! Small cracks are a simple job to repair. As a matter of fact, a whole industry was created around just such a project. It's called caulk, and second to duct tape, it's a DIYer's best friend!

Choosing the Right Tools

Be sure to choose the right caulk for your needs. It comes in different colors and several different formulas for use inside and out. I recommend looking for one that's easily cleaned up with water, is paintable and waterproof.

I accidentally used a silicone caulk on a ceiling repair once and didn't notice it wasn't paintable. Take it from me, once it sets, caulk is one of the toughest substances I know of to remove from a painted wall. Double-check those labels!

ALL CAULK GUNS ARE NOT CREATED EQUAL

I also recommend buying a quality caulk gun. A standard gun can cost as little as $5 or $6. For about $10, you can get a tool that will last for several years around your house and be a lot less aggravating to operate. It's well worth the $5 upgrade.

The difference is in the drive mechanism. The less expensive models work on a friction lever concept. After awhile the lever tends to slip. That results in uneven caulk beads and a general sense of frustration when the tool you paid good money for stops doing its job!

You should be able to find a caulk gun with a geared mechanism for around $10. The gear system operates much more reliably over a longer period of time in my experience. I've had one of these for several years and it's served me well...even after a couple falls off a ladder (the caulk gun — not me!).

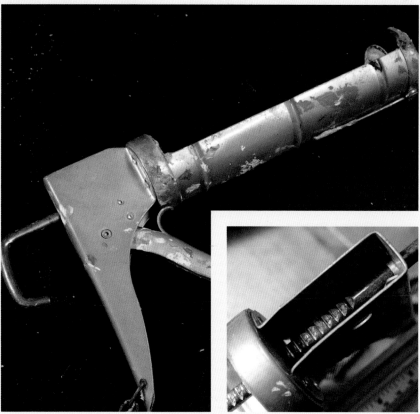

To Avoid a Mess

When you're using any caulk gun, remember to disengage the drive once you're done laying out the caulk bead. Not doing so will cause the gun to continue to operate. This can result in a messy situation on your floor or worse.

To disengage the plunger on caulk guns like this one, you simply turn the lever on the back 90 degrees.

This will turn the gear mechanism and stop the flow of caulk.

I forgot to do this once while taping a segment for a show on DIY Network. The resulting mess (fortunately, it happened out of sight of the camera) didn't go over well with the guys who had to clean it up! They have my gratitude.

Filling Small Spaces

A job well done starts with the right size caulk bead. The right size caulk bead starts with the proper cut on the end of the caulk tube. Even though my caulk gun has a built-in cutter, I prefer to use a utility knife to make the cut. The cutter on the tool gets dull over time and can mash the tip on the tube. It may seem like a small thing, but you know what they say about the details!

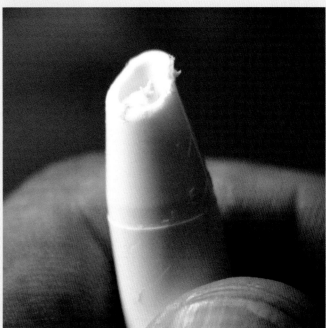

1 Cut just enough off the tip of the tube to create about a 3/16" opening in the end. It's better to cut the hole a little small and then cut more than it is to overcut the tip to begin with — for obvious reasons. A slight angle will help when it comes time to apply.

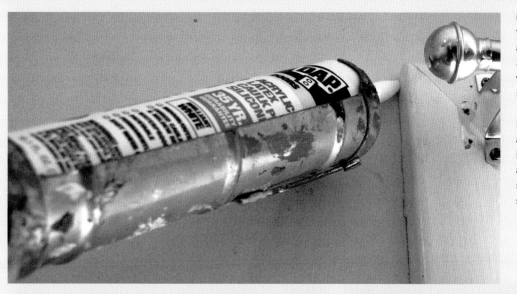

2 For the small gaps along the side of the trim, simply apply a thin bead of caulk. Start at the top of the opening with the caulk gun angled slightly. This will allow you to "pull" the bead down the trim. It should be about ⅛"-wide along the length of the opening. Squeeze the trigger gently and move the tube along at the same time, keeping an even steady pace.

Notice in the two photos above that there are gaps in the bead. This can happen if there's air in the tube or if consistent, even pressure isn't applied along the length of the bead. No worries...it's actually preferable to the situation on the right.

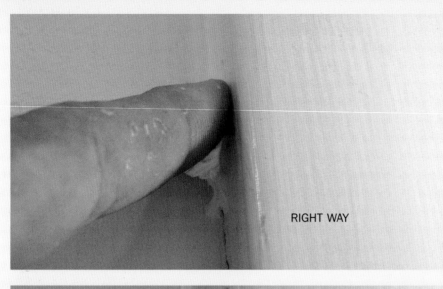

RIGHT WAY

3 Too much caulk can turn into a big mess in a hurry! If this happens, you can still use your finger as described in the next step. You'll just need to follow it up with a damp rag to remove the excess.

In either case, dampen your finger and smooth the caulk along the seam. This forces the material down into the gap to seal it. With a nice small bead, your finger will act as a kind of plow, pushing the excess caulk farther down the seam.

It's not the end of the world if you apply too much caulk; it's simply a waste of money. And the whole point of this book is to save some cash! If you really want to be resourceful, you can scoop up the excess and use it on the next doorframe or window frame.

You can use a damp rag to wipe down the repair if you applied too much. Then, use your finger again to smooth the seam.

Be sure to smooth the caulk as much as you can without wiping it all off. If you leave lumps or blobs behind, they'll be very difficult to remove after the material has cured.

NOT SO RIGHT WAY

Here's what it looks like when someone does a sloppy job and then doesn't clean it up. The culprit would be me and that doorframe is in my house. I remember the day I did the job; I was thinking I needed to wipe down the area and then the phone rang. The rest is history. It'll get fixed...someday. Meanwhile, once the caulk on your repair has dried, a little touch-up paint will make the spot look good as new.

Be sure to immediately wash any rags that you want to keep and reuse. The caulk will wash out until it cures, then it becomes one with the fibers of the rag and you've created more of a scrunge — great for cleaning the sink, but not much else.

To keep the rest of the caulk in the tube from drying out too soon, wipe the top of the tube clean and use a small piece of duct tape to seal the opening. Just fold it over onto itself to make a seal. This will prevent air from getting in and drying it out. Don't expect it to last forever like this, but you'll get a couple months' storage using this technique.

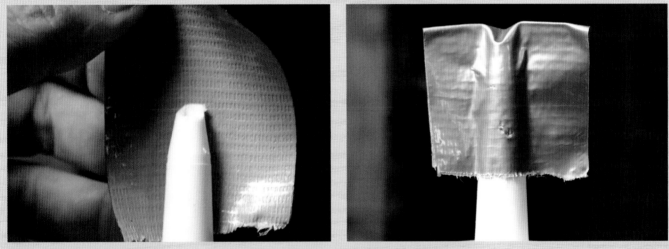

Filling the Big Gaps

For the larger gaps, spray foam insulation is the answer. It can fill a larger area than caulk and stop the airflow just as well. Be sure to use a minimally expanding version of the product or you could end up with a huge mess on your hands! The packaging is clearly marked for doors and windows, so be sure to look for it!

Also, when working with this foam, be sure to follow all the label instructions and precautions. This stuff is STICKY. That's the good and bad news. It will stick to just about any repair job. However, it will also stick to your clothes, carpet, hair...you name it. And it's not easy to get out. So, forewarned is forearmed!

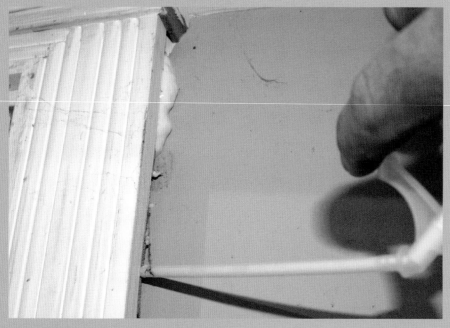

1 Protect the floor around the repair if you're inside. A perfect use for last Sunday's newspaper. Then insert the tip into the gap and s...l...o...w...l...y squeeze the trigger. You only need to fill the gap half full. The expansion of the foam will take care of the rest.

2 Here's the thing about spray foam insulation: Once you open it, you have to finish it. Once air gets down inside the tube and nozzle, the foam inside will begin to cure. Once that happens, the party's over. For that reason, you might want to have a few other things planned for the foam before you start.

Yes, I know this is a section on windows and doors, but think about that outdoor spigot that needs sealing around its perimeter. Or maybe some cable wire or plumbing penetrations into your house.

3 Wait until the foam cures (sometimes as little as 30 minutes, depending on conditions) to remove the excess. It will become firm to the touch, but won't be sticky anymore. It also yields under light pressure.

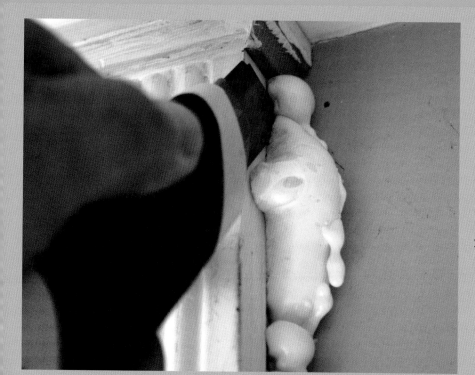

4 A sharp utility knife will trim the excess foam and leave an airtight repair. Once this area is painted, the only thing missing will be the draft that used to blow through the gap. Taking the time to fill and repair all the gaps and cracks around your windows and doors can pay off in the long run. By making these repairs, you're helping to close what's called the "building envelope." That means that your home HVAC system doesn't have to work as hard to keep the home warm or cool because less outside air is getting inside and vice versa. It's a simple concept that can truly lower your energy bills if you do it right.

Securing the Perimeter

...of your door, that is. The rule of thumb is that if you can see daylight around your door, you need some weatherstripping. Newer doors have built-in protection integrated into the door jamb itself. However, in older homes (and sometimes even those new ones), an additional layer of protection is needed to prevent drafts.

This door leads from a shop that isn't temperature controlled to the living space in the house. When the door is closed, it's clear that the gap between the door and the jamb can let air (and in this case, sawdust) into the house. That means not only is this door responsible for energy loss, but excess vacuuming as well. Taken to the extreme, that's additional electricity for the vacuum. I'm reaching, but you get the point. Sealing the perimeter of doors like this makes sense when we're trying to save energy.

1 Weatherstripping comes in different shapes and styles, but my favorite is made with a rigid aluminum bar and has a rubber gasket incorporated. It's the easiest to install and I think gives superior protection from both air and water infiltration. The rubber gasket compresses when the door is closed, effectively sealing the door to the outside elements. It's generally sold in three-piece kits — one for each side of the door and one for the top edge.

2 (BELOW LEFT AND RIGHT) The sides generally don't need to be cut for standard doors. If you find that your doorframe is shorter than the length of weatherstripping, use a hacksaw to cut through the aluminum and a utility knife to make a clean cut in the runner gasket.

3 To install, close the door and place the strip firmly against it, lining it up on the jamb molding.

4 Then use a pencil or an awl to mark the location of each of the screw holes, being sure to press the strip against the door along its length. This will ensure a snug fit. Try to center the mark in the hole as best you can. Since the holes are elongated to allow for fine adjustment of the strip (which we'll cover in a moment), it's easy to angle the pencil and get an incorrect mark.

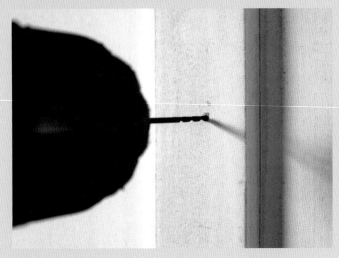

(5) Remove the strip and use a drill and a 1/16" drill bit to make pilot holes for the screws. This step will be easier with the door open.

(6) When you're finished drilling all the pilot holes for both sides of the door, line the strip up again and install the screws loosely at this point. Don't drive them all the way home!

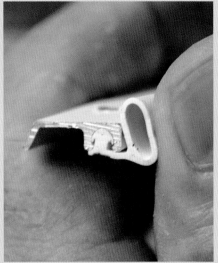

(7) Now, close the door and use moderate pressure to fit the rubber gasket snugly up against it. You want the gasket to compress about halfway. Again, this is to make sure we have a tight seal! Too much compression will eventually damage the gasket and make the door hard to close as well! Install the hinge side strip in the same manner.

8 The last step is to install the top strip. Simply measure between the two strips already installed using a tape measure. Be sure to get an accurate measurement. You want the top strip to fit snugly between the two sides. It's best to make your first cut a little on the long side and then trim from there. Once you cut it too short, you're sunk.

9 Cut the strip to length using the hacksaw and knife, then install the screws and test fit. Cut properly, the strip should fit snugly against one side and slide into place against the opposite strip with gentle pressure. Open and close the door a few times and make any adjustments necessary. If the door is too hard to close, simply loosen the screws and slide the strip away from the door slightly until it latches without too much pressure. Once the door is closed, you shouldn't see a gap between the strip and the surface of the door. If you do, readjust the strips until the gap is gone.

Closing the Gap

That takes care of three sides of the door. Now, what about the bottom? That needs a good seal as well to complete the job.

Remember, if you can see light between the door and the threshold, you have an energy drain on your hands.

Door sweeps or threshold seals, as they're called, are easy to install as well. They have the added benefit of looking (and working) much better than a rolled-up towel placed along the bottom of the door to prevent drafts.

In the photo on the right below, you can see how it works. The rubber fins create a tight seal against the wood strip of the threshold.

A metal framework with an integrated gasket fits snugly against the threshold when the door is closed. The fins adjust to any irregularities in the threshold creating a good seal along the entire width.

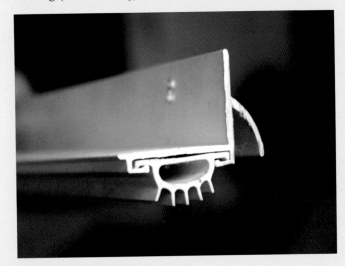

The additional drip-edge incorporated into this sweep causes any water that hits the surface of the door to roll out and away from the bottom, preventing it from wicking up inside the wood or into your home. This is the perfect style for exterior doors without overhangs, to pre- vent rain from hitting the door. On the right above, you can see what happens to a door when it's left unprotected from moisture. The laminated surface on this door has begun splitting and peeling. The drip-edge helps prevent damage like this from occurring to your door!

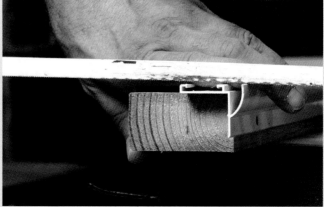

1 Drip-edges often come in several lengths, so measure the width of your door and purchase the sweep that comes closest to its measurement, without going under. Next, cut the metal frame to match the width of the door using a hacksaw. To make this step easier, try clamping the metal to a scrap piece of wood. This will stabilize the metal frame and make the cut smoother and faster.

2 Use a pair of scissors or snips to cut the rubber gasket to the same length and slide it back into the channel on the frame.

3 Next, slide the seal under the door. Hold it in place while you close the door. Be sure that the sweep contacts the threshold and that the frame clears the stops on both sides.

4 You may need to trim a small section of the drip-edge to clear the doorstop molding. That's been my experience with the ones I've installed. It's a simple cut. Just mark where the drip edge contacts the stop molding and use a hacksaw to cut a small section of the metal.

5 After removing the gasket, secure the metal to the scrap wood and make the first cut along the drip-edge side. Then, cut the metal laterally with the saw and remove the cut section. Be careful....this metal can be sharp after you cut it. Wear gloves when handling the cut edges!

6 To complete the installation, with the door closed and the sweep in place, mark the locations for the screws using a pencil. Remember to center the marks so that the pilot holes will be properly positioned to make adjustment of the seal possible. Drill pilot holes and install the screws loosely. Close the door with the seal in place. Once you've made sure the gasket is in place all along the width of the threshold, tighten the screws to secure the seal. One issue you may run into after a few weeks or months is the gasket sliding out of the metal channel. Friction can cause it to creep out over time. The simple fix is to apply a small dab of glue or rubber cement to the gasket and push it back into the channel.

7 Why go to this extra trouble instead of simply cutting the entire frame and gasket shorter? By cutting this section out and leaving the bottom intact, the frame can now fit around the molding and weatherstripping, but we haven't sacrificed any of the sealing ability of the gasket along the threshold. It's all about getting the most protection possible against energy loss! Notice how the drip edge extends all the way to the weatherstripping, giving the door complete protection against water infiltration as well!

Installing Window Film

Standing next to a window in a recently built home, you'd have a hard time telling what the temperature outside is. Modern windows are well insulated and have a slew of features that make them more energy efficient.

Stand next to a window in a home built just a few decades ago and you can really feel the difference. On a summer day, the heat and UV rays pass right through the old glass, heating up the interior of the house and fading the furniture at the same time!

In the winter, you can almost feel the chilly breeze on your skin. Older windows simply aren't designed to keep the heat and harmful rays of the sun where they belong — outside!

The real solution, of course, is to replace your old leaky windows with new energy-efficient replacement windows (how many times have you heard that ad on TV?). Unfortunately, for a lot of people, that's just not practical. And in some cases, not even necessary to accomplish the job of preventing heat buildup and energy loss.

I had window film installed in an older home I lived in a few years ago. At that time, window tinting kits were harder to find and not the easiest project to tackle, so I opted for a professional installation. The windows on the west-facing side of the house let in a ton of light and heat in the afternoon. The bedroom and office there got uncomfortably warm and I needed a quick, cheap solution.

The AC just couldn't keep the rooms cool enough, and I was tired of falling asleep at my desk! I like my workspaces nice and cool (cold, most people would tell you who've ever worked with me in a TV studio — I've seen the crew wear parkas when I was in a short-sleeved shirt!).

After the installation, the rooms were noticeably cooler. The filtered light through the tinting was actually more pleasant — not so blinding. While the tint was definitely less expensive than replacement windows, the fix still cost a few bucks. It did have the added benefit of cutting down on cooling costs, though.

Now, years later, window-tinting kits are available at just about every home improvement store for a fraction of what I paid to have it done. They're pretty easy to use and come with complete instructions. And it may just be me, but I'd swear the tint film is easier to wrangle than it was way back.

This installation is on a set of garage doors that face east. On summer mornings, sunlight blasts through the windows and heats up the garage. The heat rises and raises the temperature in the bedroom above. The quick and easy solution? Install window tint to cut down on some of that heat transference into the garage. That should keep the bedroom at least a little cooler and help cut down on the air conditioning bill.

The first step was to get the windows clean enough to apply the film. Sure, dirt acts as a nice filter for sunlight, but it gets in the way of proper adhesion!

Like painting walls and trim, preparation in this project is key. If you don't start out with a clean, clear window, your results will be less than perfect.

1 Start by using a garden hose or a bucket and sponge if your windows are as dirty as these. That'll help get the thick stuff off. Even though we'll be adding the film to the inside of the glass, this is the perfect time to get the windows their cleanest.

2 Use window cleaner and shop towels (I like them better than paper towels because they hold up better in tough jobs and don't leave flakes and fibers) to give the inside and outside of the windows a good scrubbing. Here's an old trick for tracking down stubborn streaks and smudges on windows: clean the outside of the pane with horizontal strokes and the inside with vertical. That way, when you see a mark, you can tell which side of the glass it's on.

3 (LEFT AND BELOW) Once the thickest of the dirt and grime was removed, the windows were still...dirty. You may have this problem, as well — hard water deposits and mineral buildup. Over the years, and especially if you have errant sprinklers that douse your windows, the deposits can get nasty. The solution that works best for me is vinegar. Pour some on a rag or use it in a spray bottle and give the windows a second go-over. You will see a difference immediately. The acidic vinegar cuts right through the buildup. Let it dry and repeat this step if necessary.

4 (LEFT) Once you get the glass clean, you're not done. Again, you know what they say about details. Now we need to look for specks and spots. Not much fun, but a must-do. If not removed, they'll cause lumps and bumps in the tint — not what you want! Use a razor scraper to remove any foreign material on the glass surface. Again, this is more important on the inside of the glass, but it's a good time to take care of the outside as well.

5 (LEFT AND ABOVE) The edges of the glass need special attention to ensure a smooth-looking tint. If there's too much crud in the corners, the tint could begin to peel up. To avoid that, use the razor scraper to get rid of paint and grime along the perimeter of the frame. Then use a rag to wipe it clean.

6 (ABOVE LEFT AND RIGHT) Also, be sure to look for stickers or remnants of decals that may be on your window. This one had faded so badly that it was nearly transparent and difficult to see. Because it was on the inside of the window where the tint was to be applied, it had to go! Use the scraper to remove as much as possible, then use an adhesive remover or paint thinner to get rid of the residue.

7 (LEFT) OK, so you think your window's clean enough? It's not. To make sure your film adheres as it should, use the glass cleaner that comes with the installation kit. It's designed to remove any trace residue of all the fluids and cleaners we've used to this point.

8 The kit also contains a squeegee for the final cleaning and to install the film. Hold it at a slightly downward angle and pull it from top to bottom, using moderate pressure. Work side to side until the window is completely dry. You might want to use your finger on top of the blade to add pressure if needed. The rubber blade will push the cleaning solution and any contaminants to the bottom of the window. Use a rag to wipe the residue from the window frame, then wipe the blade clean and continue.

Here's a look at the windows before and after the cleaning. What a difference! Who knew there were trees outside!

9 (LEFT) Before you start to unroll the tint, be sure you have a large, clean surface to work from. It's important to be able to unroll the film without it becoming contaminated with dirt and other foreign matter. I'm using a sheet of plywood that I've vacuumed for a clean work surface. Lay out your tools so you'll know right where to find them.

10 (BELOW LEFT AND RIGHT) Next, measure the glass in the window. Once you know the height and width, add at least an inch to those measurements. This will be the size you'll cut the tint. Cutting it larger than the window will allow you to trim it to the exact size once it's in place.

11 (ABOVE LEFT AND RIGHT) Before you unroll the tint, take a look at one corner and you'll notice a protective layer laminated to one side. We'll be removing this layer prior to installation, so it's a good idea to familiarize yourself with it beforehand. The easiest way to remove it is with two small pieces of Scotch tape. Apply a piece to opposite sides of the film and pull apart with gentle pressure. The backing layer should separate fairly easily from the tint. The tint itself is sticky to the touch. This adhesive is what holds the film to the window. Be very careful not to let the film fold over on itself and keep it away from dust and other particles that could get stuck to its surface.

12 Once you're comfortable working with the film, unroll enough to cut the first piece. In this case, we're cutting ours to about 24 inches square. Use a long straightedge to make the cut with a utility knife. The knife comes with the installation kit; the straightedge doesn't. I used a drywall t-square, but a yardstick, level or a simple length of trim molding will work. Be sure not to scratch the surface of the film when you're working with it! Use firm, even pressure when making the cut. Apply downward pressure on the straightedge to hold the film in place.

13 (LEFT) Once you've cut the tint to size, separate the film from the backing using the method described earlier. You may find it easier to have someone help you with this process. With two people, each of you can hold two corners of each layer and pull them apart evenly. Once separated from the backing, the film needs to be sprayed with the application solution, as does the window itself. Again, if you're working alone, it might be easier to simply hang the film using the taped corners. This worked perfectly in this project. I hung it below the window and was able to spray both at the same time. Be sure to hang the sticky side out!

14 Once the film and the window are sufficiently doused with the spray, carefully lift the film and apply the sticky side to the glass. Because both are wet, the film should slide easily on the glass. Get it centered on the window before moving onto the next step.

15 Spray the film again with the solution. The key to a successful installation is to keep the film wet as you smooth it using the squeegee.

16 Again, use gentle pressure to work out any air bubbles under the film. Pull the bubble to the closest edge using the rubber blade. Remember to keep the film and the rubber blade wet for the best performance.

17 Once the film is reasonably smooth, it's time for a trim. The nice thing about getting the installation kit is that it comes with a nifty little plastic gadget designed to make cutting corners easy (and a good thing in this case). It fits into each corner and has slots cut out for the blade. Just slide the razor along the slots and vo-ee-la (as a director I once worked with loved to say), you have a perfectly cut corner.

18 It also works for trimming the sides of the film along the edge of the window frame. If you don't have one of these cool little tools, you can use a credit card or small ruler.

19 Once the film is cut, gently pull the excess away. Remove the strips slowly to keep from pulling the film off the glass. Use the razor knife to cut any stubborn spots — don't try to tear the film!

20 The small gap along the edge is necessary for a couple of reasons. First, it allows for thermal expansion of the glass (yup...it moves). And second, the gap will allow you to push air bubbles out in the next step. Wet the film again and use the rubber squeegee to push any remaining air bubbles out. You can move from side to side, or up and down, or a combination of both to move the air bubbles to the nearest exit. Just be sure to get all the air out and be careful not to shift the film on the window.

21 The good news is....we're done with one window! Now, only 7 more to go in this project. Here's what the final comparison looked like on this garage. What a difference! I love projects that give you immediate gratification. It makes all the work worth it. Plus, this project can lead to real energy savings when it's done. According to the manufacturer of this film, it's designed to last upwards of 10 years, making it a very worthwhile investment in time and money.

Insulating a Water Heater

One of the easiest ways to save money on your energy bill is to stop heat loss from your water heater. If it sits in a space that isn't climate controlled, your water heater can be a big drain on your wallet. Typically, a water heater insulation kit costs under $25, but can pay back big dividends simply by keeping the heat inside the heater where it belongs! The water heater shown here sits in the corner of an unconditioned garage/basement. Because of its location, it has the potential to cost the homeowner money simply by losing heat to the outside air, especially in the cold winter months. It's the perfect candidate for a blanket of insulation!

Water heaters installed in temperature-controlled spaces are less likely to lose energy through heat transference, but they can still benefit from having additional insulation!

Above is a standard-size insulation blanket available at most stores that stock insulation. It measures 48" long by 75" wide. It will be perfect for our project.

① First, measure your water heater top to bottom to make sure you purchase a blanket that will fit. Since the tanks come in different shapes and sizes, it's important to have the information on hand when you go to the hardware store.

② Lay the blanket out on a clean surface to cut it to length. You'll need a straightedge — I'm using a drywall square — and a sharp utility knife. Be sure to orient the blanket so that you're cutting the proper dimension. It's a good idea to test fit the blanket so that you know you'll have enough material to go all the way around! I've made this mistake in the past, and this is a perfect time to remember the old adage: "Measure twice...cut once!"

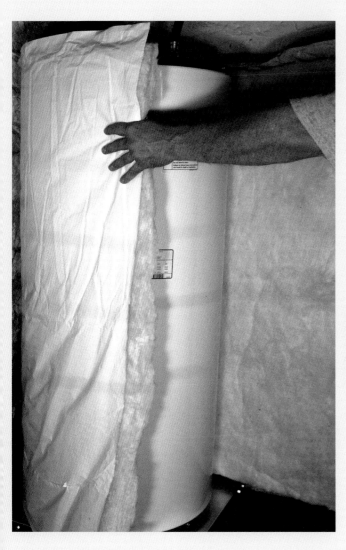

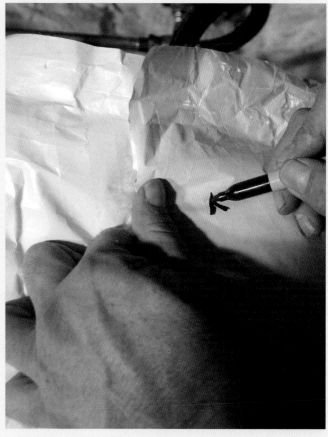

③ It's also possible that you won't have to cut any off the length, so again, be careful on this step! Once the material is cut to length, wrap it around the heater and mark the spot where it overlaps itself. Be sure not to pull the blanket too tight. The insulation needs to remain in its "expanded" form to properly insulate the tank.

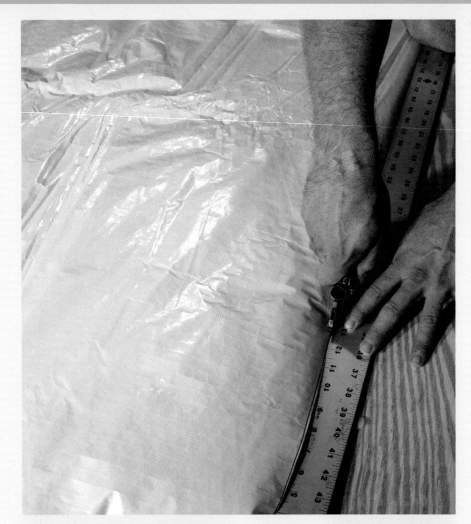

4 (LEFT) Then, lay the blanket out on the clean surface once again and use the straightedge to cut the width along the edge where you made the mark. Again, be careful to keep a consistent line along the entire length of the material.

5 (PHOTOS BELOW) Once the blanket is cut to the proper width, again wrap it around the heater and use two or three short pieces of tape to hold it in place. A piece at the top, halfway down and near the bottom should do the trick. During this step, make a mental note of where you'll need to cut around the thermostat access panels and overflow valve. You might even want to make a small mark on the outside of the blanket to help you remember where they're located. Once the blanket is in place, it can be difficult to remember where those cutouts need to be!

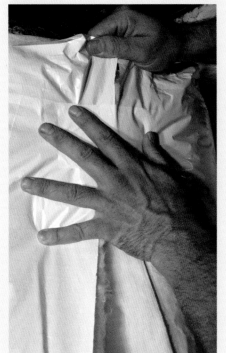

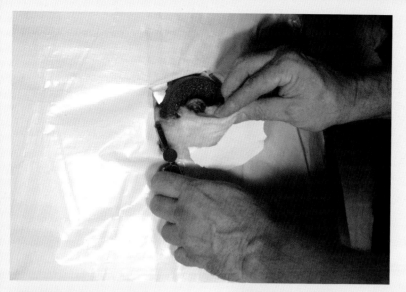

6 Now, locate the overflow valve and use the utility knife to cut the insulation around it. Use just enough pressure to cut through the jacket and the insulation and cut within a half inch or so of the valve. Don't worry if the cutout isn't perfect. It just has to be functional and allow access to the valve. Notice that we're installing the blanket on a newly installed heater. It doesn't have the overflow tube installed yet, which makes wrapping the blanket around the tank much easier. If your tank has the overflow installed, be sure to slide the blanket underneath the pipe.

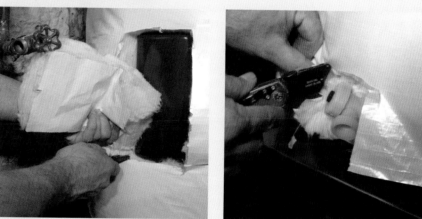

7 (PHOTOS ABOVE) Next, cut the blanket around the thermostat access panels. You should trim the blanket to clear the panels about a half inch on each side. Again, neatness isn't crucial here, but do your best! You may also have to cut around the drain valve at the bottom of the tank, depending on how large your tank and blanket are. Just use common sense.

8 (LEFT) When you're done, the blanket should look something like this. Your heater may have only one thermostat access panel, in which case you'd have one less opening.

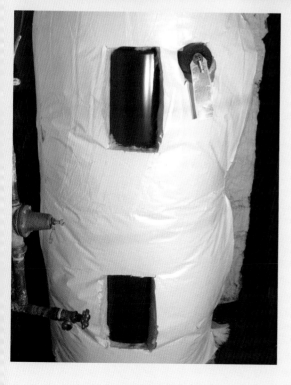

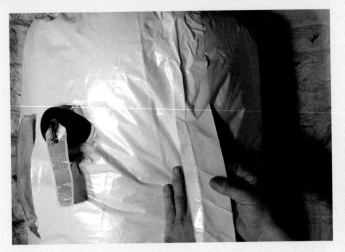

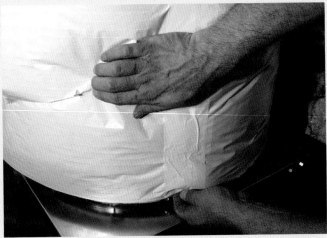

9 Once all the cutouts are complete, it's time to secure the seam on the side of the tank. Gently pull the two sides together and use a length of tape long enough to run the entire height of the blanket, closing up the seam. This step might be easier if you have a friend helping. One of you can hold the seam closed while the other applies the tape. If you have any favors to call in, this may be the time to do it! You'll find out who your real friends are!

10 Finally, to secure the top of the blanket to the tank, you can simply fold the jacket material over itself and tape in place. I like to make the installation a little neater by cutting slits about every 6" along the top of the tank, creating flaps. Then each of the flaps will fold neatly onto the top of the tank, where you can tape them in place.

11 If you have excess insulation left over from your initial cut, you can use it on the top of the water heater to add an additional layer of protection against heat loss. Otherwise, you can consider your work here done! If you listen closely, you can almost hear the money you're saving by keeping those energy dollars hard at work inside the tank!

Insulating Water Pipes

Now that you've completed the first step in saving money by making sure your water heater has the proper winter coat (it works just as well during the summer, by the way), let's move on down the line, so to speak.

Think about it...the water that's been heated in the tank is all set to move to your bath or kitchen faucet — through cold, uninsulated pipes! That means all those energy dollars you just saved could be disappearing into thin air. The good news? There's a pretty easy way to keep that from happening, or at least cut down on the amount of energy lost while the water reaches its destination.

Depending on where your pipes are located, it might be a good idea to insulate both the hot and cold water lines. That's especially true if the pipes are in your garage or crawl space and you live in an area where cold winter temperatures might cause the pipes to freeze. This is one of the least expensive insurance policies you can buy.

We'll focus on the hot water line coming from the water heater in this project. If you decide to do your cold water lines, it's the same process.

There are a couple of different options when it comes to foam pipe insulation. My favorite has built-in adhesive strips in the seam. The adhesive is covered by protective plastic that is easily removed once the insulation is in place. Don't make the mistake of taking this plastic off before you install the tubes. Once it adheres to itself, it can be tougher than Krazy-Glued fingers to get unstuck!

We'll tackle the pipe one section at a time, measuring and cutting lengths of insulation to fit perfectly.

1 Measure the length of the pipe coming from the top of the water heater. Since we're mitering the joints, you'll need to measure just beyond the union of the two pipes. The photo on the left above gives you an overall view of the pipes we'll be insulating. On the right, you can see the first section that we'll be working with.

2 We measured and cut a section of insulation that would cover the joints at each end of the short section. The insulation is easily cut with an ordinary pair of scissors or a utility knife.

3 Notice we cut this piece at a 45 degree angle so that it would form a miter joint when the next piece is attached. You don't have to get out the miter gauge to get the exact measurement. A good old-fashioned eyeballing should do the trick.

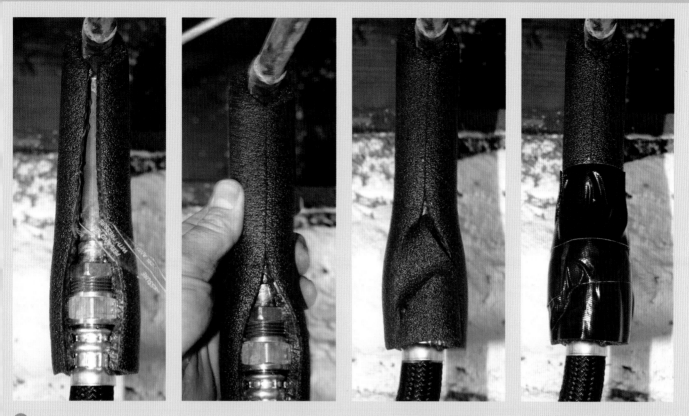

4 The next step is to slip the insulation around the pipe. Once it's in place, grasp the protective plastic covers and remove, then press the two adhesive sides together for a snug fit. Notice in the second picture that the insulation does not completely wrap around the pipe union. The simple solution is to use the scraps left over from the miter cut and place them in the gap. If oriented correctly, they should fit almost perfectly. Once in place, wrap the area with duct tape to secure in place.

5 Next, measure from the miter you just completed to the end of the pipe, or at least to the next joint if it doesn't continue in a straight line. Then cut and install another section of insulation in the same manner as the first.

6 To secure the joint, use a strap of duct tape over the top of the second piece of insulation and down the sides of the first. This will lock the two pieces together to prevent the joint from slipping.

7 Since our water heater is in the garage, we decided to insulate the cold water supply line as well. The process is the same, but here's a trick when it comes to connecting insulation at 90 degree angles for a clean, professional look. Cut a small section from the length of insulation where it meets the 90 degree joint. This is easily done with a pair of scissors.

8 Then, cut the insulation that will be butting up to this piece in a "V" shape. Again, a simple cut with scissors. Note that the adhesive strip runs along the long side of the "V." This will allow it to more easily fit over the valve stem on the line, visible at the far right in the photos below.

9 Finally, another short piece of duct tape will keep the joint from separating. Remember that the entire length of pipe in exposed areas needs to be insulated for the job to be effective. It's a simple project that, when combined with insulating your water heater, can really add up in energy savings over time.

Installing a Programmable Thermostat

One of the simplest, least expensive and fastest ways to start saving energy dollars immediately is by installing a programmable thermostat to control your home's HVAC system. Not only can it take the bite out of high utility bills, but it can actually solve arguments over who gets to control the temperature of the house. OK, that last point may be a stretch because someone will still have to decide what temperature to set the thermostat to, but from there, it's "set it and forget it!"

A programmable thermostat saves money by preventing the wasteful use of energy to cool or heat your home when nobody's there. In the winter, you can set the thermostat to a lower temperature overnight, saving you the cost of heating the house while everyone's asleep. Personally, I love a cold, dark bedroom to sleep in, but in the morning, it's nice to get out of bed to a warmer room.

Basically, the thermostat can think ahead for you and begin to heat the house an hour or so before you get up. That way, you wake to a nice, comfortable home. At night, about an hour before you're ready for bed, the thermostat can turn the heat down to let the house cool gradually.

In the summer, the opposite is true. While you're at work, the thermostat automatically raises the temperature of the system so you're not paying to cool a home that no one's enjoying. But it'll make sure you come home to a cooler house by starting the cooling process before you get there.

It all works through the magic of electronic circuitry, and the best part is — you can buy one for under $40 that'll do everything you need it to! That money can be made up in no time by saving you those wasted energy dollars.

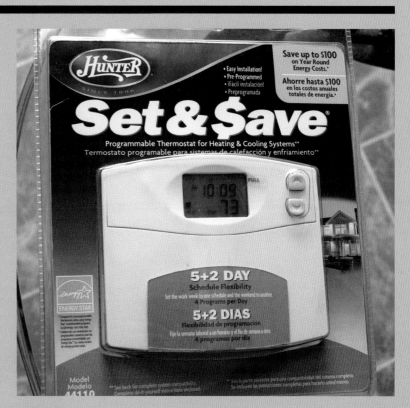

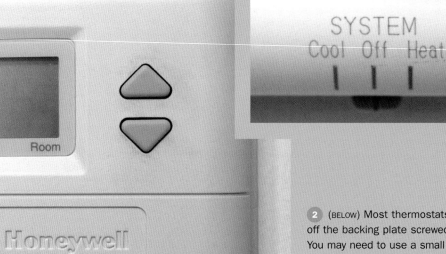

1 To begin, locate your home's thermostat and set it to the "Off" position. Wait until you hear the unit shut off if it was running.

2 (BELOW) Most thermostats simply snap off the backing plate screwed to the wall. You may need to use a small screwdriver to pry it from the plate. Be gentle, though, to avoid breaking the small wires connected to the unit. In some older homes, the wires may be attached to the thermostat itself instead of the connection shown here. In any case, they all work to send signals to the main HVAC unit to trigger it On and Off.

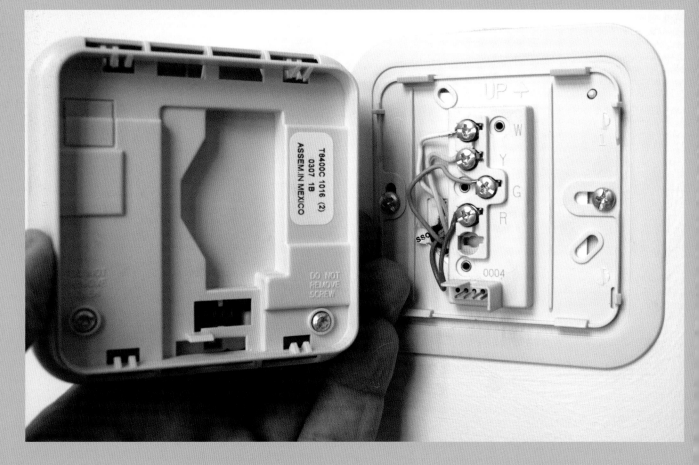

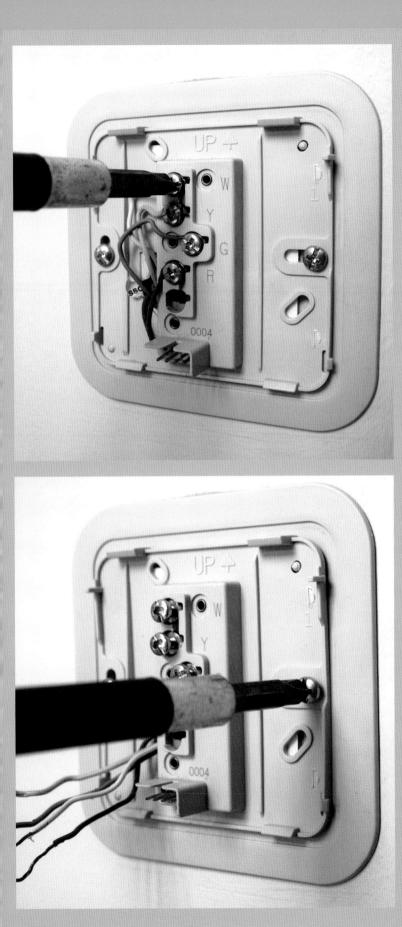

3 Next, remove the screws holding the wires to the wall mounting plate. Be sure to note any markings on the terminals and which colored wires were connected to each. It's a good idea to take a digital picture at this point in case you need to refer back to it. If the thermostat you purchased came with wire coding stickers, use them at this point so you can readily identify the wires during the next few steps.

4 There will likely be two or three screws that need to be removed and these should be fairly obvious to your eye. Once you have removed them all, gently pry the mounting plate from the wall. You might need to score around the outside of the plate to cut through any paint buildup. Don't force the plate off or you could end up with a drywall repair job at the same time!

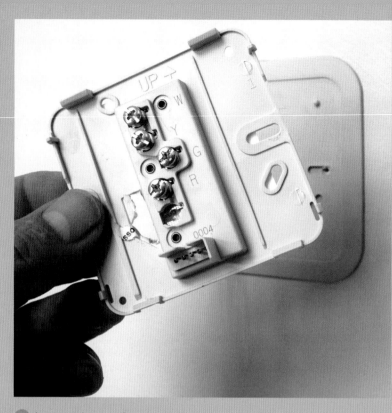

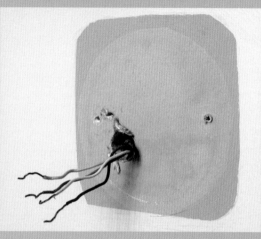

5 In our project, we found a dual-plate system (above). Both need to be removed. That left us with some paint touch-up to do. You may find yourself in the same boat, but this is the best time to tackle that side project so you don't have to remove the new thermostat to make the repair!

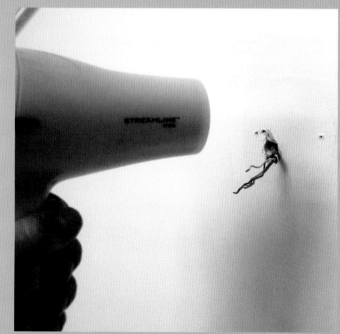

6 A hair dryer will help dry the paint faster and speed up the job.

7 (RIGHT, BELOW LEFT AND RIGHT) Next, follow the instructions that came with your new thermostat by installing the new mounting plate. Align it on the wall, pull the wires through the appropriate opening and drill a pilot hole for the mounting screws. If you're lucky enough to hit a stud, you won't need to use wall anchors. You can use a small level if you absolutely, positively have to have the plate perfectly level on your wall. However, I'd say trust your eye and you should be able to get it close to perfect without one! Then, install the rest of the mounting screws.

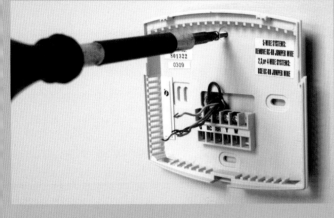

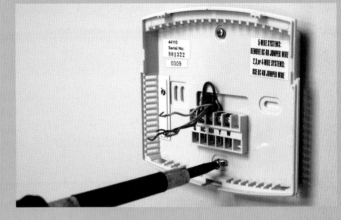

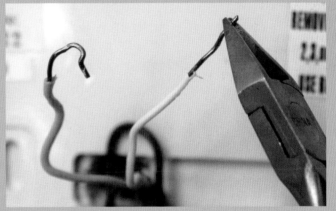

8 (ABOVE LEFT AND RIGHT, LEFT) Once all the screws are installed, it's time to reconnect the wires. Your new thermostat will have detailed instructions on where to connect them, but the new unit will likely have color-coded terminals that match the colors of your existing wires. You may also need to straighten the wires for some terminals with a small pair of pliers. These small gauge wires are easily broken, so be gentle during this step, especially if there's not much wire to work with coming out of the wall.

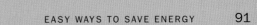

9 Once all the wires are connected, the next step is to make any necessary adjustments on the internal controls of the thermostat. One of the most important adjustments to be made is setting the "heating energy source" switch to the correct position. If your heating system uses gas, the switch in this case needs to remain in the "HG" position. If your system utilizes electricity for the heating function, the switch must be slid to the "HE" position. If you're not sure which type of system yours is, be sure to call a professional to identify it before completing the thermostat installation.

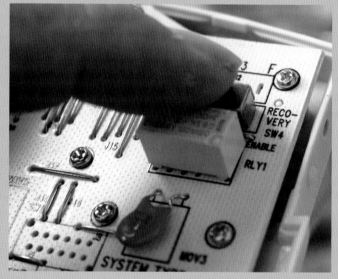

10 Finally, some programmable thermostats today offer a "Recovery Mode" option. Basically, this allows the thermostat to gradually change the temperature in your home, rather than trying to make the change all at once. The logic behind the feature is simple — think of it in terms of driving a car. You've long heard the lessons about not making "jackrabbit" starts when you drive. They waste gas. The same is true for your HVAC system when it needs to make a temperature adjustment in your home. Making the change gradually will, in theory, use less energy than trying to make the temperature jump all at once. Now that you know the reasoning, just be sure to check the instructions on your thermostat and look for the small switch on the back. Set "Recovery Mode" to the "Enable" position to avoid those jackrabbit temperature changes. The switch simply slides into place with light pressure. My suggestion is this: Try the thermostat in "Recovery Mode" for a couple of months and then disable the function for another couple. If you see a difference in your utility bills, you can decide whether or not you want to utilize the feature.

11 (ABOVE AND RIGHT) Once the thermostat is set to your liking, it simply snaps in place on the mounting plate. Usually, it slides over mounting studs along the top of the plate, then gentle pressure is used to finish the installation.

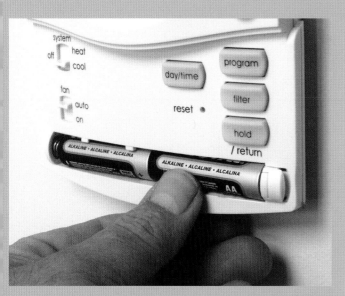

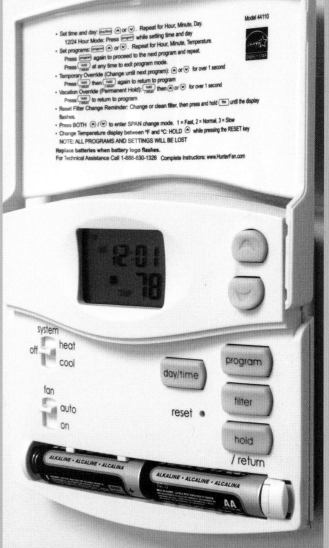

12 (ABOVE) Next, lift the front cover and install the correct batteries. Be sure to note which way to orient the polarity to avoid any possible damage to the unit!

13 (RIGHT) Finally, you can program the thermostat now and let the energy savings begin! And don't be intimidated by all the buttons and numbers. Most thermostats like this one give you the option of having one schedule throughout the week and a separate schedule on the weekend. That way, since your home is more likely to be occupied more hours during the day on the weekend (unless you're a workaholic), you can set the program to make fewer changes. In other words, once it begins cooling or heating the house in the early morning hours, it doesn't necessarily have to make another temperature change until you retire for the night.

Installing a Motion Sensor Light Switch

"Turn off the lights when you leave a room!"

How many times did we hear that as kids or yell it as parents? Not sure I know how to count that high, really... Not that it ever made any difference when it was yelled at me, anyway! I'm betting it was somebody's whizbang engineer of a dad who finally got fed up and invented the motion sensor light switch. What a brilliant idea!

The truth is, turning off the lights in an unoccupied room saves energy and saves money. That's the bottom line. Dead men tell no tales and dark bulbs use no energy. So, if you're sick and tired of yelling at the kids or simply forgetting to flip the switch yourself, this is your dream project!

A motion sensor switch works by sensing changes in heat or movement in a room. It can tell when someone has walked into a space and immediately turns the lights on. Once the room is empty, or at least until the device senses no more movement for a period of time, it can be set to turn the switch off.

Usually switches like this come with just about everything needed for the installation and well-detailed instructions for less than $20.

Also, be sure to check the packaging to make sure the switch will control fluorescent light fixtures. Some are designed specifically for this purpose, while others can actually be damaged or damage the light fixture if installed.

Most switches of this type allow you to set the sensitivity to movement so that small pets don't run around turning your lights on in the middle of the night. They also allow you to set the duration of their "On" time. Most range anywhere from five minutes to an hour.

Think of them not only in terms of saving energy, but of offering you convenience. Your hands are full with groceries, boxes, kids, you

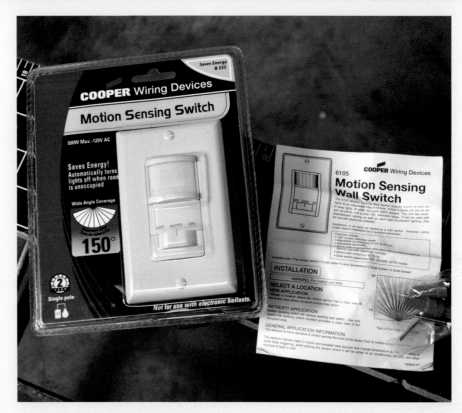

name it...and the motion sensor switch will automatically turn the lights on for you.

Installing one of these in a walk-in closet is a great idea. Even a kid's playroom makes sense. I installed this one in a storage area of my shop. That way, I don't have to yell at me for leaving the lights on!

1 The first step in this project is to turn the power to the circuit off at the breaker panel. Then, use a piece of painter's tape as a sign to anyone who might accidentally turn the breaker on while you're working. Better safe than sorry!

2 (ABOVE) Then, turn the switch to the "On" position. Most likely, if you turned off the correct breaker, the lights won't come on. That's good. But not enough precaution! The next step may seem unnecessary, but when you're working with electricity, it's wise to work with the Department of Redundancy Department. Unlike plumbing, where finding out you accidentally left the water on in the middle of a project can cause a horrible mess and cost you some cash when things get soaked, discovering you left the electricity on can cost you your life. Okay, let me jump down off my soapbox and let's continue.

3 (ABOVE AND LEFT) Remove the two screws and the switch-plate. Next, remove the two screws holding the switch to the electrical box. Although the power is "presumably" off, be very careful not to let the screwdriver slide into the area where the wires are connected to the switch. Again, better safe than sorry.

4 Next, gently pull the switch out and away from the box, exposing the wires attached to it. Be gentle pulling the switch out. Sometimes, there's very little excess wire to work with inside the box — don't force it and risk breaking a wire.

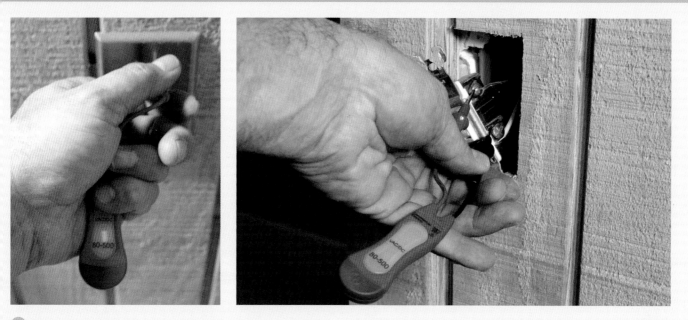

5 Use a circuit tester to make sure there's no current running to the switch before moving on to the next step. There are a number of different testers available. This one is simple to use. Just touch the probes to the appropriate wires and if electricity is present, a small lamp will glow in the tester, as you can see in the photo on the left. Since the lamp remained dark (photo above) I'm confident there's no electricity running through the switch.

6 The next step is to loosen the terminal screws holding the wires in place. Also, remove the ground screw if one is present. It will be a bare copper wire attached to the grounding terminal of the switch. Once I removed the switch from this box, I found the ground wire tucked in the back of the box. Someone had done some sloppy electrical work in the past. It's amazing the mistakes and shortcuts you'll find others have taken when you start tackling home improvement projects. The nice thing is that you get the satisfaction of knowing you corrected the problem and truly made an "improvement" over a potentially unsafe situation!

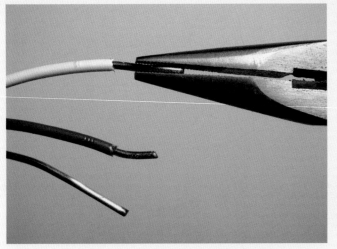

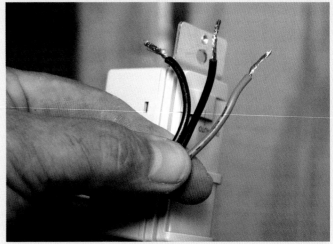

7 Next, be sure each of the wires is bent straight and that the black and white wires have only about one half inch of bare copper showing. Use a pair of pliers to straighten the wires if necessary.

8 The new switch has 3 wires attached. One of them is the ground wire and the other 2 connect to the hot and neutral (black and white) wires.

9 Twist the green ground wire together with the bare copper coming from the electrical box. Use a wire nut to secure the connection. The next step is the extra mile I like to go every time I'm working with electricity. You can never be too rich, too good-looking or too careful when it comes to electrical current. To prevent the connections from coming apart inside the box and posing a potential hazard, I like to wrap each connection with electrical tape. Because electrical tape is rather elastic, it tends to pull back on itself when wrapped around an object. Because of that tendency to stretch back to its original state, wrap the connection in a counterclockwise (looking down at the top of the wire nut) direction. This way, it will tend to tighten the connection rather than working against it. Be sure to wrap both the nut and the wires, thereby giving the connection another layer of security against coming loose.

10 Repeat this process with the remaining two wires, being sure to follow any special instructions that came with the switch!

11 Next, tuck the wires back into the electrical box and press the switch into place. Use the screws from the old switch to secure the new one if there were no screws in the new packaging.

12 Before installing the cover, check the instructions that came with the switch. You'll find a small cover on the front that when removed, reveals the controls for sensitivity and duration. You need to decide what settings are best for your application. I generally have the lights in my storage area shut off after about 5 minutes. That seems to be plenty of time to get in and get out.

13 Once you've made the adjustments, replace the panel and install the switch cover using the screws provided. Turn the switch to the "Off" position and turn the breaker to the circuit back on. Then set the switch to "Auto" and watch your energy savings add up! You may find that you need to adjust the settings on your switch after a few days. You can fine-tune it so that it fits your needs perfectly.

Sealing Outlets & Switch Plates

They seem so small and innocent, but in larger numbers, outlets and switch plates can be energy thieves.

Think of each one as being a hole venting directly to the outside of your home...and it could be as big as half an inch! When you add up the number of outlets and switch plates in your home and think about the fact that air can pass through those little openings, letting both drafts inside and store-bought air outside, you can see that closing off all those little leaks might be a smart thing to do!

The key to solving this problem is sold in packages that contain enough insulation material to do a number of outlets or switch plates. They're inexpensive and easy to install. All you need to do is pop out the perforated pieces and slide them into place. It's literally a three-step project, and identical for both a switch or outlet, so I've mixed the steps together on the following pages.

1 Remove the cover screws (two for switch plates, and one in the center for outlets). As always, be careful when working around electrical boxes, being sure to never put the tip of the screwdriver near the wires attached to the sides of the switch or outlet. Doing so could give you a nasty jolt! Remove the cover itself and set aside.

2 After removing the perforated cutouts on the insulation, place the insulation sheet over the outlet in the wall. It should fit snugly and remain in place without having to be held. A tight fit ensures maximum air leak stoppage!

3 The last step is to simply replace the cover and put the screws in. I recommend doing this simple 3-step process on all your exterior wall electrical boxes.

Insulating Garage & Basement Walls

It's been said that the two biggest reasons for insulating a garage are comfort and cost.

First, adding insulation can make a noticeable difference in that area year-round. It will be warmer in the winter and cooler in the summer. If you spend any time at all in the garage tinkering on cars or projects, the added comfort level is worth the effort.

Second, the cost of this project is minimal given the benefits in return. It could eventually even pay for itself in energy cost savings if done properly.

There are a few different scenarios we'll cover on this project:
1. Exposed-stud walls
2. Cinder block or concrete walls
3. Rock foundations/walls

In all cases, remember that the insulation should not be left exposed, but covered with drywall or plywood. Check your local codes for any special requirements.

Choosing the Insulation

Insulated walls are most common in garages. They're generally 2×4s, but some builders use 2×6s when building exterior walls, so be sure you know what size you're dealing with before you buy the insulation.

A 2×4 stud wall (actually only about 3½" deep) will accept R-13, while 2×6s (actually about 5½" deep) will allow you to install R-19 insulation.

Calculating the amount of insulation you'll need is pretty simple as well. Measure the height of the wall (generally 8', but yours could be taller) and multiply it by the length.

If your garage is 24 feet deep, you'll be covering a total of 192 square feet along one wall. Each package of insulation will indicate the area it will cover, so from here on, it's just simple division.

The roll of R-13 at the right will cover 45 square feet, so it would take 4¼ rolls to do that wall.

Choose faced insulation for this project. The vapor barrier will help prevent moisture from transferring through the wall.

Finally, choose precut for standard walls. If your walls are taller than 8 feet, get the continuous roll. You'll be able to cut the insulation to the proper length for a perfect fit.

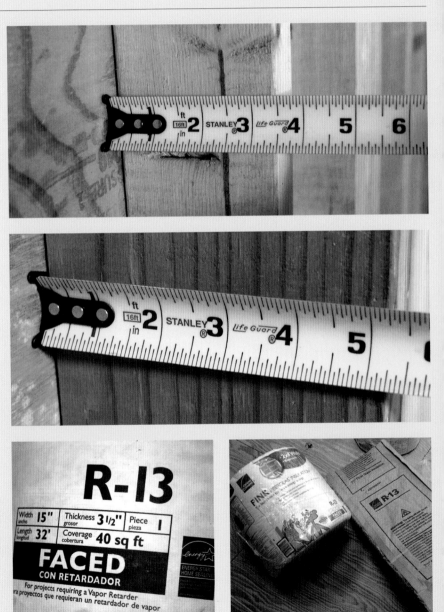

The Right Tools

In addition to a stepladder, you'll also need a good staple gun. Traditional staplers apply pressure to the back of the gun, while forward-action staplers allow you to put the pressure directly over the staple being driven. This is my preferred tool, but not everyone likes them, so be sure to test-fire one in the store before purchasing. Quarter-inch staples are usually adequate.

You'll also need a utility knife and a straightedge to cut the insulation to length or width when necessary. If you don't already have one, buy one with a retractable, replaceable blade system. You can usually get one for around $5-$10. A straightedge can be something as simple as a scrap of wood, as long as it's a little wider than the insulation.

Finally, be sure to wear all the protective gear recommended by the insulation manufacturer. That includes gloves, long-sleeved shirt and pants and a dust mask. These will protect your skin and lungs from the irritating fibers that may become airborne when installing the insulation.

Exposed-stud Installation

Most older garages and unfinished basements are likely to have exposed-stud framing. The reason is simple; the builder saved money by leaving the walls unfinished. Ironically, you can save some money (on energy) by insulating and finishing them yourself. The process is really very simple, and the savings (and added comfort) is well worth the time.

1 If your garage has standard eight-foot exposed studs, the job is relatively simple. Unroll the insulation and press it into the wall cavity, starting at the top. Pull the paper tab over one of the studs and staple it in place.

2 Fold the other tab onto the adjacent stud and staple. Don't stretch the facing too much or it might tear. Then work your way down the length of the insulation, lightly pulling any wrinkles out of the facing and stapling it into place about every foot.

3 Repeat this process on each wall cavity, folding the tab over the one next to it and securing it with staples. Use a hammer to flatten any staples that don't seat correctly. This will help avoid tearing the facing when installing the next batting.

Cutting Insulation

You'll need to cut the insulation to fit into narrower or shorter spaces, such as areas above doors and windows. Don't try to stuff a full-width piece of insulation into a narrow cavity, as it will lose its insulating properties — it needs to fully expand to do its job correctly.

To cut the insulation, lay it out flat on a work surface that won't be damaged by the razor knife. A scrap of plywood works well. Use the straightedge to compress the insulation and draw the knife toward you in several passes. Don't try to cut all the way through on the first draw. Also, be sure to make a clean cut through the vapor barrier — don't try to tear it.

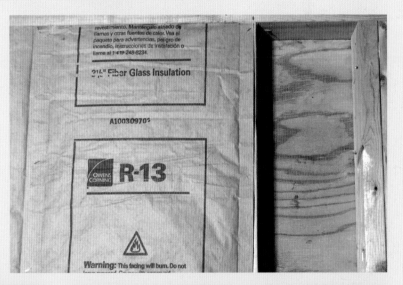

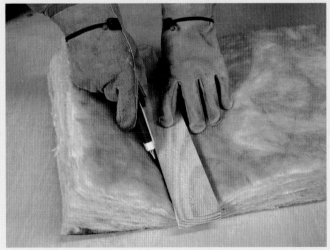

Cinder Block or Concrete Walls

Often, basement and garage walls are block or poured concrete. In these cases, you need to "fur" the wall. That means simply adding studs that will hold the insulation. There are a couple different ways to accomplish this.

First, determine whether or not you should waterproof the wall. This is a good idea, especially if the wall is below grade (underground). That's often the case with basement walls, although houses built on sloping ground can have at least one basement wall that isn't underground.

In any case, if there's noticeable moisture coming through the wall, apply a good coat of waterproofng before continuing. I prefer the oil-based versions over the water-based, despite the odor and cleanup. If you have any doubt about whether or not the problem can be remedied, call a professional and have it checked.

While furring can be installed with concrete screws, specialized tools will make the job easier and faster.

Powder-actuated fastening tools use a small amount of gunpowder to shoot a fastener through the stud and into the wall. Inexpensive models are available for as little as $30, and heavy-duty versions like this one made by Hilti can be rented for about that same price on a daily basis.

While using wood studs is fine in most situations, I was introduced to a product called EcoStud while doing product reviews for HGTVPro.com Weekly. It's made from recycled resin and is impervious to moisture and insects. Dimensionally the same as a standard 2×4 wood stud, EcoStuds are great for a project like this.

The EcoStud is secured in place with construction adhesive and concrete fasteners. A flange along its entire length has predrilled holes for the fasteners. The studs also have precut locations for running electrical or plumbing lines.

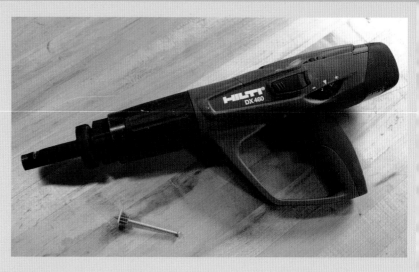

Be sure to use ear protection when using tools like this and always read the instructions prior to operation!

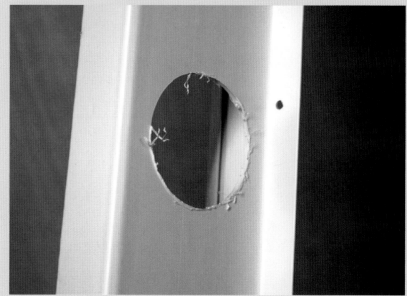

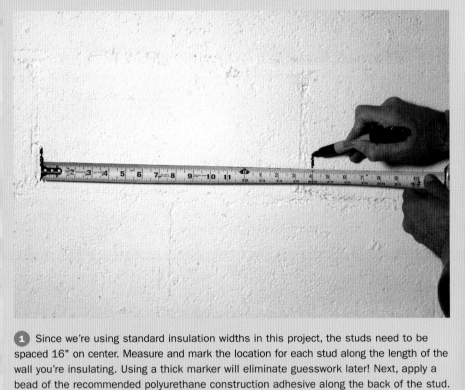

1 Since we're using standard insulation widths in this project, the studs need to be spaced 16" on center. Measure and mark the location for each stud along the length of the wall you're insulating. Using a thick marker will eliminate guesswork later! Next, apply a bead of the recommended polyurethane construction adhesive along the back of the stud.

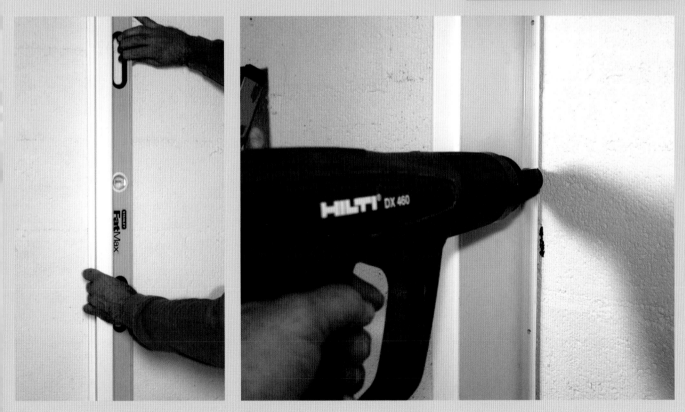

2 Hold it in place on the wall at the first marked location. Use a level to be sure it's plumb.

3 Install at least three or foiur fasteners along the length of the flange.

4 Once you've installed the studs along the wall, you can begin the insulation process. The manufacturer designed the EcoStud for use with spray-foam, rigid, or fiberglass insulation. The only difference in the installation process is the recommendation that packing tape be used instead of staples to secure the vapor barrier.

Rock Foundations

This presented an interesting dilemma for the homeowners when they decided to insulate their garage. It's a situation you may run into as well. I'm offering a brief outline of the procedure here. Since every situation is different, you may be able to take some of these techniques and apply them to your project.

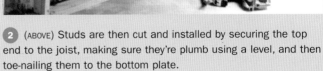

1 After removing the old shelving and debris along the wall, a pressure-treated bottom plate is installed. It needs to be far enough from the wall's surface to allow the installation of studs between it and the joists above. The bottom plate is secured with the same concrete fasteners as used in the cinder block wall.

2 (ABOVE) Studs are then cut and installed by securing the top end to the joist, making sure they're plumb using a level, and then toe-nailing them to the bottom plate.

3 (LEFT) Once all the studs are secured, the insulation can be installed and covered with drywall or the material you choose. I prefer plywood in areas like this, as it gives you nearly unlimited storage options. Nails or screws can be installed anywhere, and plywood is capable of holding more weight than drywall.

Preventing Molehills from Becoming Mountains

I'm sure you've heard the expression before — "You're making a mountain out of a molehill." That's what this section is all about — small problems that can get nasty really quickly if they're not remedied early. It's common sense and much easier to solve a problem when it's smaller rather than larger. Take, for instance, a nail hole I found protruding from the roof of my home (there are pictures in the first section). Had I checked and repaired the situation early on, I wouldn't have had the problem of wet and disintegrating drywall on the ceiling of the spare bedroom. Now, I have two problems to fix. You get the idea. The worst thing you can do with a small needed repair is ignore it!

Filling Cracks in Concrete

I was working with some guys I'd hired to do some concrete work around my house one day when one of them said, "Concrete is gonna do two things — shrink and crack." And he's right — you can lay money on it. The key is to fix the cracks before they become large problems.

Here's how it works: Cracks allow water to seep under the concrete surface to the substrate below. Then when it freezes, the water turns to ice and expands, causing pressure below and making the crack larger. Let that cycle continue long enough and you'll have a huge expense on your hands. It's a good idea to get right on the fix as soon as you see the problem.

Below is what can happen when you ignore cracks in concrete. Seeds get inside the crack and begin sprouting. Soon you have a miniature garden growing on your patio. The weeds and grass begin to grow, causing the cracks to widen. Before you know it, you're faced with a huge repair bill!

The patio on the right will likely have to be completely demolished and re-poured. Once the cracks have spread that badly, it's difficult to make any repairs that will last.

The first step is to take a good, close look at your concrete surfaces. Whether it's a patio, walkway or porch. The key is to locate and identify cracks early on. And don't forget to check the area where the concrete surface meets the wall of your home!

Let's divide the repairs into two categories: Small cracks (less than ⅛") and large cracks (more than ⅛").

Small Cracks

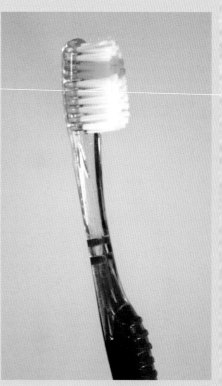

1 The first step in repairing small cracks in concrete is to clean away any loose debris. An old toothbrush makes a great tool to clean up the small pieces of concrete that can inhibit a good repair. One with stiff bristles works best.

2 If there's dirt in the crack, use a garden hose to rinse it thoroughly.

3 A shop vacuum is a good tool for removing stubborn chips and rocks that may be lodged in the bottom of the crack. This is also a good alternative to using the hose if you need to repair the crack in a short time. No need to wait for the concrete to dry!

4 Once the crack is cleaned and dry, you're ready to make the repair. There are several products from which to choose. Some can be poured directly into the crack (like the product on the left), while others need to be squeezed or set in a caulk gun. I've found that for really small cracks, the tube variety is the best choice. The caulk gun can force the material into the crack easily.

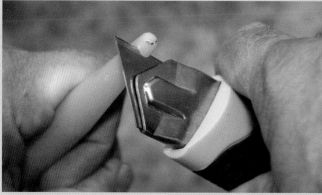

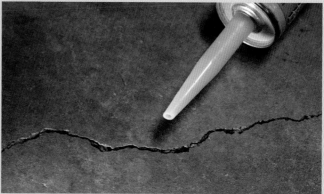

5 Cut the tip of the tube at a slight angle to make it easier to control. Don't make the opening too large for the size of the crack. A small ⅛" opening should do the trick. If you find that not enough of the sealer is coming out or it's too difficult to squeeze, you can always enlarge the opening.

6 Gently squeeze the caulk gun trigger as you pull the tip along the length of the crack. Since the sealer is self-leveling, you can overfill just slightly.

7 For slighter wider cracks in the small crack category, try using the pourable product. It has a tendency to seek its own level and seep more readily into the crack. Some of the same rules apply. Cut the tip of the container at a slight angle to make pouring more manageable.

8 Slowly pour the repair material into the crack. Again, since it's self-leveling, you can mound the material just slightly, but be careful not to overfill or you'll have a mess to clean up!

9 Continue pouring the solution into the crack along its entire length. If you find that there's a little too much product sitting on the surface, use a small putty knife to smooth out the lumps.

10 Once you've smoothed the rough spots, try using an old sponge to clean up the area around the crack. Avoid removing too much of the repair material from the crack itself or you'll be defeating your purpose! Still, this is a good way to make the repair look a little tidier. The cured material will help prevent water, dirt and plants from making the problem worse in the future!

Larger Cracks

1 Many of the same rules apply to repairing larger cracks in concrete. The problem area needs to be clean, dry and free of debris. A wire brush comes in handy to clean out the larger areas. You can sometimes find this type of brush in discount stores for under a dollar. It's a great item to have in your toolbox! Try angling the brush to give it more grip along the edges of the crack. This way, it will dislodge any small pieces of concrete that may be hanging on by the proverbial thread.

2 Once you've dislodged any debris from the crack, use a garden hose to clean it completely. Allow any standing water to dissipate before continuing to the next step. Since we'll be using a concrete re-surfacing product to fill this crack, it's not necessary to let the area dry completely.

3 I like using this repair product on larger cracks because it also serves as a great underlayment for resurfacing. It blends more readily with the surrounding concrete and it's always been a durable fix in my experience.

4 You'll also need the following tools: A trowel. It doesn't have to be large or expensive. You can pick up a light-duty trowel for a couple of dollars at some discount stores. A nylon brush. This is commonly used for wallpaper projects. Since I can't stand wallpapering, I've found other uses for this tool! A putty knife for smoothing out small spots — and it makes a great mixing tool!

5 Since we need to mix the repair compound, here's a little trick for getting the measurements correct — especially for small jobs. Use a sharp knife to cut a plastic water bottle roughly in half. Recycle the top and save the bottom as a measuring cup.

6 The resurfacing product calls for a ratio of 7 parts powder to 1 part water. Since the repair we're making won't require that much, let's use 3.5 parts powder to ½ part water — make sense? Pour the powdered repair material into a container — an old coffee can or paint can should hold enough for a few repairs.

Be sure it's clean to start. Pour 3½ measures of the powder into your mixing container. Then add ½ measure of water and stir. You may need to add more water, but do so a little at a time. Mix with a putty knife or wood scrap until there are no visible lumps or dry powder.

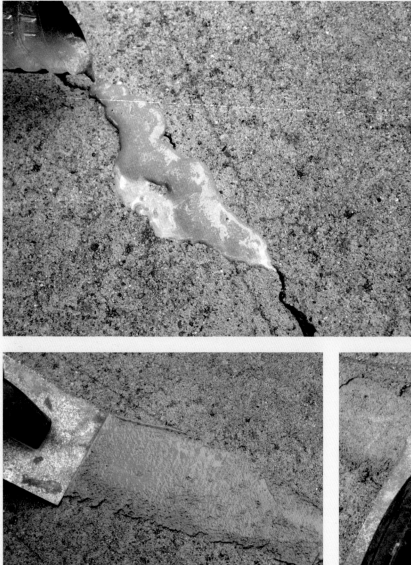

7 Once you have the mixture to the proper consistency (thin enough to pour, but not watery), use the bottle to scoop some out of the container. Then begin pouring the compound slowly into the crack.

8 (ABOVE LEFT AND RIGHT) You can work small stretches at a time. Pour the compound into the crack, then use the trowel or putty knife to smooth it into the crevice.

9 (LEFT) Work the compound from two angles. Smooth it along the length of the crack, then turn the tool to a 90-degree angle to be sure it forces the repair material into the space. Continue this method along the length of the crack.

10 When you're finished troweling, use the nylon brush to lightly smooth the entire repair. This will remove any excess material and result in a more finished look.

11 You'll see that using the brush really blends the repair into the surrounding area. There's no invisible fix for concrete, but since I'll be re-surfacing this entire area, it's not a great concern. The important thing is that water will no longer be running underneath this slab causing damage!

Repairing Spalled Concrete

Literally, spalling means "to chip or break off into smaller pieces." In masonry, spalling is the top surface of concrete or brick "popping" off. It's often caused by the freeze/thaw cycle in winter. Older brick is very susceptible to the problem because of the way it was made. It has a tendency to absorb water more than modern brick does.

In much the same way, unsealed concrete will absorb water and weak areas will tend to break away when the water freezes. This can also be due to chemical weaknesses in the concrete mix when it was poured.

Spalling looks a lot like craters on the moon. For bricks, the only real solution is to remove and replace the brick. Luckily, concrete is a much simpler fix!

It should be repaired as soon as possible to prevent further erosion of the concrete surface. Once there's a place for water to puddle, it won't be long before that tiny little pit becomes a much larger problem!

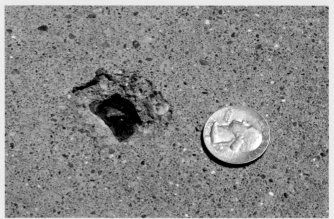

1 The first step is to remove any debris from the hole. It needs to be clean before the repair can be made. A small whisk broom works well. In this case, I like to use an old wallpapering brush. This is an invaluable tool for a number of projects. Brush as much of the dirt and debris out as possible.

2 One of the easiest ways to get the dust and dirt out of the area is with compressed air. If you don't own an air compressor, just use a product like Dust-Off or other canned air. I used to think buying cans of air was a little silly, now I use them all the time in repair projects. They're much easier to use than dragging a compressor and hose around for small fixes.

3 Now, rinse the area with water to get all the ground-in crud out. This will remove any stubborn particles that brushing or blowing missed.

4 (ABOVE AND RIGHT) Once the damaged area is clean, mix up some resurfacing compound as described in the section on repairing cracks and pour a small amount into the depression. Use the trowel to work the mixture into the area. A couple of passes should do the trick.

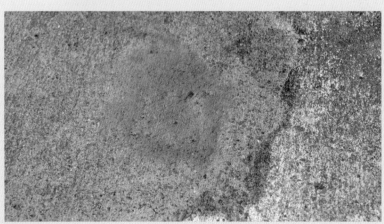

5 (LEFT AND ABOVE) Finally, use the brush to smooth out the final repair. This also helps blend the repair into the surrounding concrete. Don't use too much pressure with the brush, you just want to create a textured surface to match the surrounding area. Note: Most patio or walkway surfaces will have a textured finish to prevent slipping. If you're working on an area that has a slick or smooth surface, just use the trowel to smooth the material to match.

Spalled Steps

The edges of concrete steps will sometimes crack or chip as well. It's important to repair these areas to prevent further erosion from happening. Can you say "legal liability"? I knew you could. Fix it as soon as possible!

1 First, follow all the ealier instructions for cleaning the area thoroughly. Then, use a cinder block or piece of wood that extends above the top of the step. If you use wood, just place a couple of bricks behind it to hold it in place. This will create a dam to hold the repair material in place.

2 (ABOVE AND RIGHT) Mix the repair compound and pour enough into the area so that it overflows slightly.

3 Once the cavity is filled, use the trowel to smooth the material and feather the edges smooth. The cinder block will provide a crisp edge for the repair. Use the brush to lightly smooth the patched area, again matching the surrounding surface. Avoid stepping on this area until the product cures fully, according to the manufacturer's instructions. It's also a good idea to seal the entire surface to prevent further damage to the area. Just be sure to use a sealer designed for use on masonry surfaces!

Repairing Mortar Joints

Mortar is the glue that holds the universe together, or at least the bricks that make up the universe.

Over time, mortar can get damaged by the freeze/thaw cycle or plants that cause it to simply disintegrate.

Whatever the reason, if you catch the problem early enough, you can prevent it from becoming a true money pit! Once the mortar has deteriorated to something like the images below, I'd recommend getting a professional to take care of the problem.

Eventually, this sort of damage can lead to monumental problems, like entire walls collapsing. Granted, these are extreme examples and took years to occur, but they're simple enough to prevent if caught early!

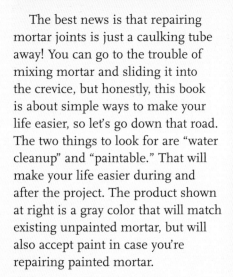

The best news is that repairing mortar joints is just a caulking tube away! You can go to the trouble of mixing mortar and sliding it into the crevice, but honestly, this book is about simple ways to make your life easier, so let's go down that road. The two things to look for are "water cleanup" and "paintable." That will make your life easier during and after the project. The product shown at right is a gray color that will match existing unpainted mortar, but will also accept paint in case you're repairing painted mortar.

1 (ABOVE AND RIGHT) Once you've identified the problem area, clean it out with compressed air. Again, if you have an air compressor, that's great, but a can of Dust-Off works fine. Be sure to wear safety glasses to keep small chunks of mortar or dust from getting into your eyes. Voids like these can be caused during the construction process. The mason may simply not have put enough mortar into the area. They can also be the result of improperly mixed mortar deteriorating over time. Whatever the case, it's best to remove any foreign debris from inside the hole that might prevent the repair from adhering.

NOTE: Be sure you're not filling "weep holes" in the brick façade. Weep holes are generally round and found near the bottom of a wall, close to the foundation. If you see a number of them in a pattern, don't attempt to repair them. Their job is to let any moisture trapped between the brick and the exterior of the wall escape to the outside!

3 After a couple of minutes, the mortar will begin to stiffen up somewhat. Use an inexpensive chip brush to lightly brush the mortar repair along the mortar line. This will help blend it into the surrounding area and make it less noticeable. Use just enough pressure to smooth out the repair, but not so much that you push the repair material too far back into the crevice.

2 Next, use the mortar repair caulk to fill the void completely. Make sure it's overflowing just a bit, but not too much.

4 Once it dries, it'll be hard to see the difference between the repair and the real mortar next to it!

The damaged area in this picture is a settling situation. The lower half of the wall has settled while the upper portion has remained in place over the course of a couple years. If you see areas like this around your home, you need to have a professional look for the reason the settling is occurring. The problem could be much larger and need immediate attention. The benefit of repairing a situation like this is that the repair material is flexible, so if the bricks move, the repair will move with it.

Mortar cracks like this are very common in areas with clay soil that has a tendency to expand and contract. The resulting cracks tend to open and close during the course of the year, depending on the amount of rain and the freeze/thaw cycle.

Again, if you have cracking in mortar joints that continues to get worse, call a professional immediately to keep the problem to a minimum. Otherwise, this is a great fix that won't break the bank and will keep things tidy, weather-resistant and nearly invisible!

1 If it's determined that the area is stable, you can proceed with the repair in the same manner as shown earlier by first applying the caulk repair...

2 ...then blending with the brush.

Installing a Spigot Shutoff

Hose bib, water spigot, hosepipe...whatever it's called in your neck of the woods, just about every home has one. And they're usually located about 10 feet away from the "perfect spot." But that's a different story.

The thing with a bib/spigot/hosepipe is that if you live in an area where temperatures drop below freezing, it can and will freeze during the winter months. Not a huge problem (after all, who really wants to wash their car in January anyway?), until you consider that if it freezes to the point that the pipe inside the wall cracks, it can be the source of a lot of emotional distress. You can translate that into "big repair bill" in most cases.

Sure, you can install one of those Styrofoam covers you'll find at the home improvement store, but this only offers a little protection. Now, if that's the only option open to you, that's great, but if you have access to that pipe that's running either under your house, through the garage or the basement, there's a much better insurance policy available. It can cost less than $10 (for PVC) to about $25 (copper pipes).

It's simply a shutoff valve that you install inline that allows you to turn off the water to that spigot only. No water to that spigot means nothing to freeze and make the pipes burst. You get the idea.

The valve above is for PVC plumbing and costs about $7. The one on the right uses new technology for copper plumbing and runs a little less than $20.

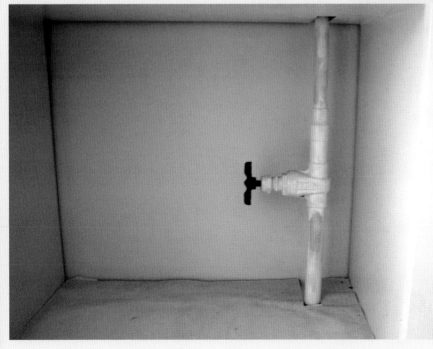

1 (LEFT, BELOW LEFT AND RIGHT) The first step is to determine whether or not you have access to the pipe that feeds the spigot. Locate the spigot in question and go to the interior of your home on the other side of that wall. Remember, by interior, I also mean crawl space (I hope you don't mind dirt and bugs because it'll be stocked with both, most likely). You'll need to be one-part home inspector and one part private investigator. Locate an area that you can work in and that gives you access to the water line for about a foot and a half. In most cases, this isn't a problem. In this example, the line came into my shop through the foundation and followed the wall to the floor joists of the room above. Perfect! Remember, you need to have reasonably easy access to this spot each winter to operate the valve.

2 Now, before you make another move, turn off your home's main water supply. Failure to do this would be disastrous (and very wet), to say the least. There may be a couple of options on this step. There should be a main shutoff somewhere in your home. It could be in a closet, the basement (hidden in a corner), or some other spot that you could spend hours looking for. This main shutoff is located in a downstairs bathroom's closet. A word of warning — sometimes these twist valves can get a little finicky over time. In other words, they get clogged with mineral deposits and rust. If yours is in bad shape, use the next method to turn off the water. If you turn a nearly broken valve, you could end up with a much larger headache than you expected!

3 The water shutoff located near the curb in front of your house is often the easiest way to stop the flow. Check with your water utility to make sure they allow consumer operation of the valve. In most cases, you should be fine. Shutting off the water requires the use of T-handle wrench like this one. Most homes have one of these lurking somewhere in the garage. If not, contact your local water utility. You'll also need a hefty standard screwdriver or prybar to remove the top from the water shutoff if yours is underground.

5 Once the lid is off, look for a valve inside. Turning this valve 90 degrees (it may turn only one way) will shut off the water supply to your home. The top of the handle is most often configured to line up with the valve's orientation. Leave the handle on the valve until your project is done as a reminder that the water has been turned off!

4 The cover should be marked clearly. Be very careful when opening this lid — it's extremely heavy and can easily smash a finger. Gloves are in order if you're in doubt.

6 Next, inside your home, open the highest faucet. In other words, if your house is 3 stories — open one on the third floor. Also, open the lowest water outlet in your home — most likely the outside spigot that you're working on. This allows the pipes to be evacuated of the vast majority of water. You'll likely still have water released from the pipe you're working on when you cut it, but it will be minimal.

Copper Pipe

In the past, this would have been a messy, time-consuming job. Thanks, though, to the new technology I spoke of earlier, it's much easier. These new fittings are called Gator Bites (there is another similar product called SharkBites). The beauty of these fittings is that they don't require any "pipe sweating." In other words, you don't have to solder them into place. They are held together with "gripped compression," for lack of a better term. Given the choice, I'd take this route every time!

Another advantage to this new style of fittings is that the company also offers a removal tool. It simply compresses those black rings you see in the photo to release the pipe. Brilliant!

Your water line is either ½" or ¾" in diameter, so purchase the correct fitting for your pipe size.

You'll also need a copper pipe cutter. They're available for under $10 at the hardware store.

A small cutting wheel inside the pipe cutter (at left) slices through the copper when the tool is rotated around the pipe. The thumbwheel lets you adjust the pressure of the cutter. Don't try to cut through the pipe in a single pass!

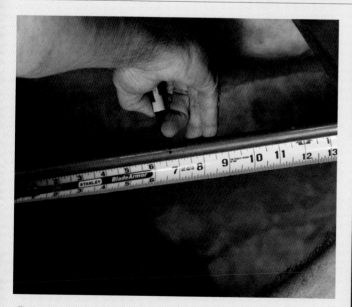

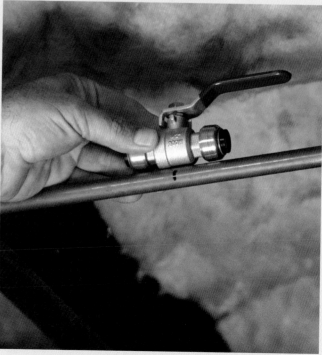

1 Measure and mark the center point of the pipe between the joists. Placing the shutoff directly between the joists will provide enough room for you to get your hand into the space and operate the valve when needed.

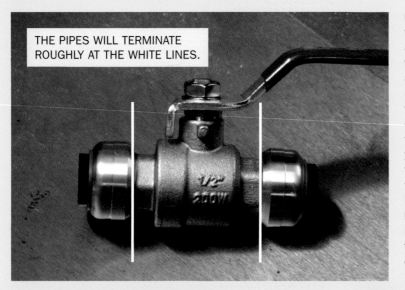

THE PIPES WILL TERMINATE
ROUGHLY AT THE WHITE LINES.

2 Remember back in school when you thought math was stupid because it could never possibly apply to anything you'd ever do in the real world? Guess what...? We can't simply cut this pipe in half, stretch it apart and slide the valve in between. That could put undue stress on other fittings down the line. Instead, we need to cut a small section from the pipe — just enough so that both ends, when inserted into the new fitting, will seat properly. To get this measurement, you'll need to know how far into each end of the valve the fitting will go. The instructions that come with the fitting should specify the insertion depth. By measuring the length of the valve and subtracting the combined insertion depth measurements, you'll know how long a section of pipe to remove. The center section between the white lines in the photo at left is the length of the section of pipe that needs to be removed.

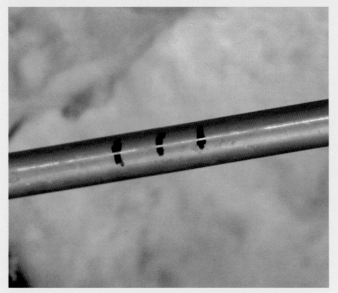

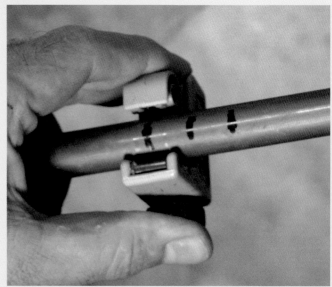

3 Once you have the magic number, simply make a mark on either side of the center line on the pipe. Before cutting the section out, make sure the pipe has ample support on both sides of the cut. You don't want one side falling completely down. There should be pipe hangers or clamps in place along the length of the water pipe. If not, simply use a clamp to hold the pipes up while you're working! Use the pipe cutter at both outside lines. Tighten it slightly onto the pipe and give it one full turn. Then, tighten again and repeat. Continue this process until the blade has cut completely through the pipe. Note: Even though you shut off the water, there will still be some coming from the pipe. Have a bucket and towel ready to catch the drips if you don't want them all over the floor or ground below!

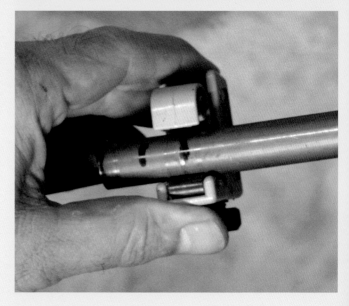

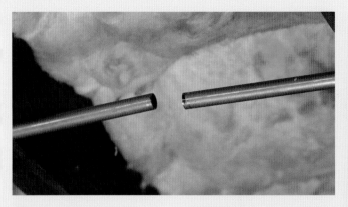

4 Once the section of pipe is removed, use emery cloth or sandpaper to lightly remove any copper fragments that may remain on the cut areas. Be careful, as the cut ends of the pipe can be very sharp!

5 When the burrs have been removed, it's time to install the valve. Using firm pressure and following all the instructions that come with the valve, press it onto one end of the pipe, making sure the handle is in the correct position.

6 Finally, once the pipe has seated completely on one side, gently push the pipes apart, just enough to slide the other open end into the fitting. Be very gentle at this stage to avoid putting undue pressure on fittings farther down the water line!

With the installation of the valve complete, turn the main water supply on. Check for any leaks and re-seat the pipes in the valve if necessary. That's all there is to it!

You'll also need to slowly open all the faucets in your home to allow the air to escape from the pipes. Do this one faucet at a time.

PVC Pipe

For PVC pipe, you'll need a hacksaw or recipro-
cating saw with a fine-toothed blade, sandpaper
or emery cloth and PVC primer and cement.

The steps for PVC pipe are identical except
that we'll be gluing the valve into place. That
means that once it's there, it's staying there
and will have to be cut out. There's no easy
removal tool when it comes to PVC.

① Once you've found the center mark on the pipe and
measured to each side, use the saw to cut away the
center section. Be sure to have towels and a bucket
handy for any leftover water in the line.

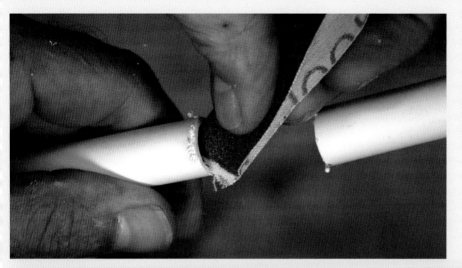

2 (LEFT AND BELOW) Once the section is removed, use sandpaper to remove any debris left by the sawing process and lightly remove the sheen from the first inch or so of the pipe's outer surface. This will allow the glue to get a stronger grasp. Gently remove any rough edges from the pipe's interior as well. Try to keep from pushing debris back into the pipe.

3 Repeat this process on the valve's interior walls, too. Removing the sheen from the PVC's surface will help ensure a leak-free connection. Rolling the sandpaper into a tube will make it easier to insert and roll around the inside of the valve.

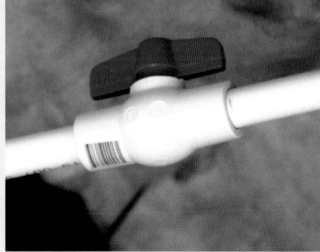

4 Now, do a dry fitting of the valve to be sure it will slide onto both ends of the pipe. Decide exactly where you want the valve to be, as you'll get about 5 seconds to change your mind once the glue is applied.

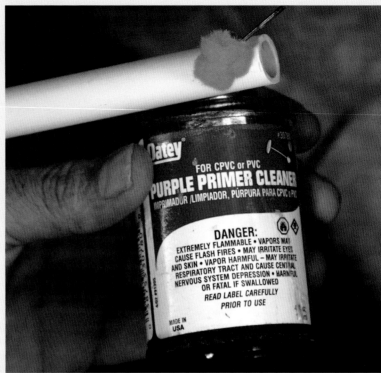

⑤ Once all the surfaces have been roughened slightly and you've tested the fit, apply a thin coating of PVC primer to the inside of each end of the valve and around the perimeter of each pipe end.

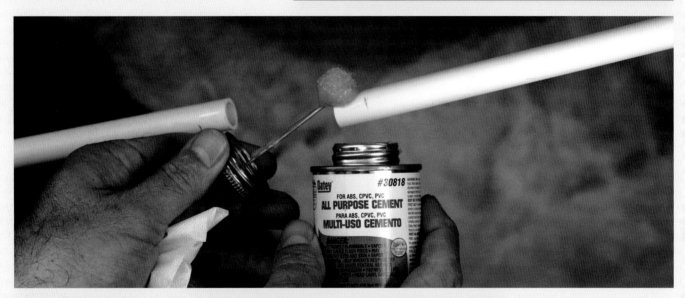

⑥ Next, apply a generous coating of the PVC cement to the same areas. You don't want so much that it's running off the pipe ends in a stream, but a little dripping is fine. Make sure all surfaces are coated!

7 (RIGHT, BELOW LEFT AND RIGHT)
Next — and do these things in one smooth motion, because when that cement sets, there's no going back — slide the valve onto one end of the pipe with the valve facing 90 degrees away from the position you want as its final. Then pull the pipes apart enough to slide the valve onto the other end. Snug everything up together and turn the valve 90 degrees to the position you've chosen.

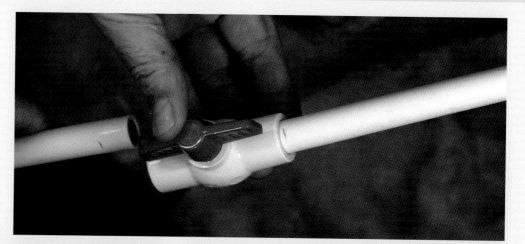

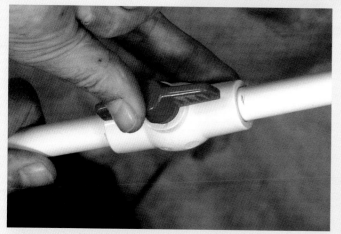

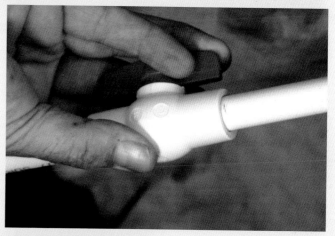

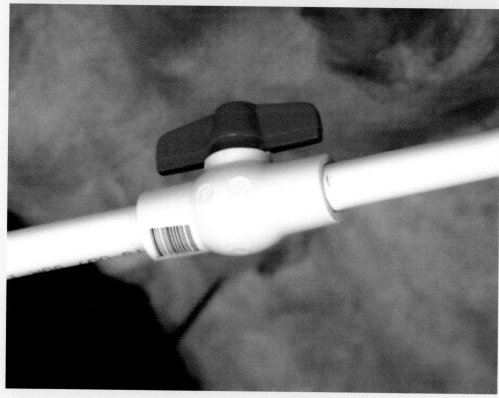

8 (LEFT) Once you're finished, it should look something like this. The difference between the PVC and the copper pipe is that you need to wait until the cement cures before turning on the water and pressurizing the system. Generally, a couple of hours will do it, depending on the outside temperature. This isn't a job you want to do on a freezing or sweltering day. Read the label directions on the cement for that manufacturer's recommendations. Remember to check for leaks once you've turned the water back on and then test the operation of the valve.

Re-caulking a Tub or Shower

This is truly an easy way to prevent a molehill from becoming an expensive mountain. The little bead of caulk where tub and shower walls meet the tub itself is the last line of defense against mold, mildew and rot inside your home's walls.

Give the area a good inspection. If the caulk bead is cracked or missing, water could be flowing behind the tub walls and into the framing of your home. If it's on an upper floor, it could be leaking onto a ceiling below.

Because the caulk bead had voids, water was able to penetrate the subflooring below this tub. It will likely have to be removed and replaced. No, that's not cheap! But it is preventable.

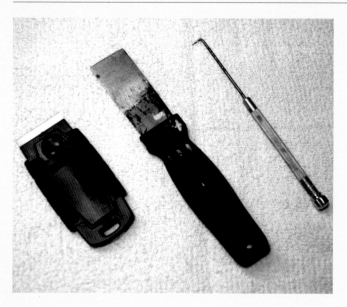

1 The first step in the repair is to remove clutter from the work area. If there is one, take the shower curtain down or roll it up onto the curtain rod to keep it out of the way. Get rid off the shampoo bottles, old sticky bars of soap and anything else that might get in the way of the job. Then you'll need to gather a few tools. This is the fun part! I like to use a putty knife, a razor scraper and dental tools. Sounds strange, but they're pretty handy for a lot of jobs! Even stranger sounding, you can pick them up at most automotive stores. You'll also need a razor knife, some painter's tape and tub and shower caulking in a caulk gun. Some paper towels or old rags are a must as well. This project can get a little messy, but it's water cleanup, so all is good!

I like my putty knives to be a little sharper than they are off the shelf. Over the years, I've learned that by cleaning them on occasion with a belt sander, the leading edge can be sharpened to an almost knife-like edge. Of course, you have to be more careful using it at this point, but a sharper putty knife lets you remove a lot more material in a project like this one without gouging the tub! You can also sharpen a putty knife with a palm sander, it just takes longer.

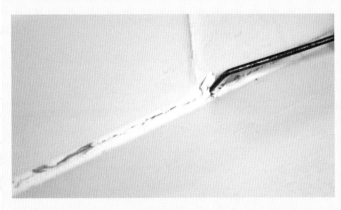

2 Using a combination of scraper, putty knife and dental pick, remove all of the old caulk from the perimeter of the tub. Try using the dental tool first to pop out loose sections of the caulk.

3 The sharpened putty knife will also help greatly in breaking any bond the old caulk has on the tub. Keep it at a low angle to help prevent marring the surface. Use your other hand to pull away the caulk as it's released.

4 Use the tool on both the horizontal and vertical surfaces to get underneath the caulk.

5 The razor scraper is good for removing stubborn areas of caulk and mineral or soap deposits that have found their way into and around the sealant. Again, be careful not to gouge the tub surface by holding the scraper at a low angle and applying only enough pressure to scrape away the gunk.

6 Once you've removed the big chunks of caulk from the perimeter of the tub, use a vacuum to get rid of the small stuff. You could wipe it away, but using the vacuum helps ensure that the little pieces won't end up under the tile during the process! With the area reasonably clean, it's time to clean it some more. It's all in the prep work, just like painting!

7 Next, use a rag and some rubbing alcohol to wipe away any residue left behind. Make sure you clean the tile as well as the tub surface at least an inch back from the corner.

8 If you notice any areas in the grout or under the tile that may be harboring mold, use a bleach-based cleaner to clean them out. An old toothbrush also helps scrub away any mold. Be sure to open a window when working with cleaners like this!

It's a good idea to fill your tub with water before applying the caulk. The tub you see in the photos is fiberglass and has some flex to it. When weight is added, it can actually move, creating a larger gap between the top surface of the tub and the bottom tile. When we apply the caulk, we want the opening to be at its largest. That way, we're sure to use enough of the caulk to fill the largest possible gap. If the caulk is applied without the added weight in the tub, there's a chance that once it's cured and weight is added to the tub (water or human), the caulk could stretch, crack and split.

9 The next step is optional and takes a bit more time, but it's my favorite method of making sure I have neat, straight caulk lines on the finished job. Place strips of 1½" painter's tape on the wall and tub about ¼" from the corner. Do this along one end of the tub to start.

10 There's no need to get out a ruler or straightedge, just place the strips by hand so they're relatively straight within ⅛" or so. Once they're in place, do the adjacent wall, overlapping the tape at the corner.

11 Use a razor knife to cut the excess tape in the corner and peel it away. Again, don't worry if it's not perfect. Just get it pretty close.

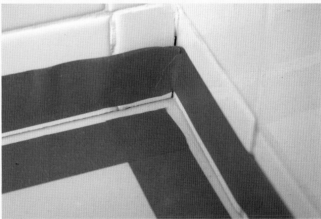

12 Repeat this process again for the third wall in the bath or shower so that you have a complete "frame" for the caulk the entire way around.

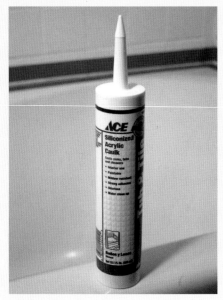

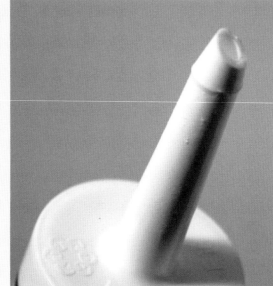

13 Next, we'll be applying the caulk. Look for a tub and tile caulk that resists mold and mildew and can be cleaned up with water. Cut the tip at a slight angle, creating an opening in the tip about ¼" in diameter. One of the biggest mistakes users make when working with caulk is cutting too much off the tip and creating an opening that allows too much product out when the trigger is squeezed. Remember, you can always cut the hole larger, but you can't make it any smaller!

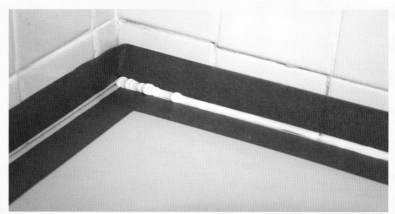

14 With the caulk tube inserted into the caulk gun, start in the corner and begin applying the caulk into the channel created by the tape. Neatness isn't a real big factor here (that's the tape's job), so don't get overly obsessed. Just apply enough to cover both vertical and horizontal surfaces. Do an entire wall at a time, drawing the caulk gun slowly and steadily toward you for best results.

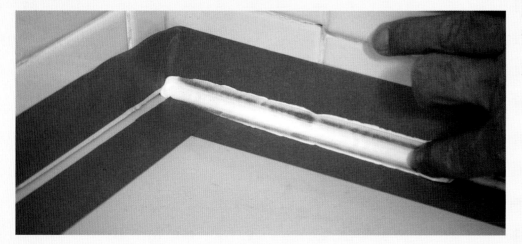

15 Then dampen your forefinger with water. Start in the corner and use your finger to smooth the caulk along the entire wall. Use light, consistent pressure along the entire length of the caulk bead.

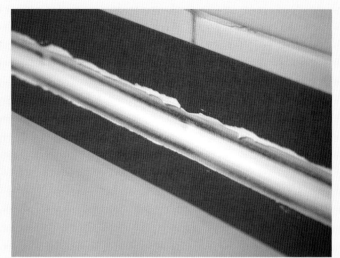

16 It should look like this when you're done. Notice there are no voids in the caulk and it has overlapped onto the tape all along the wall.

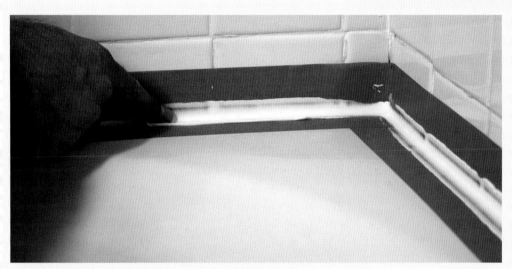

17 (LEFT) Apply sealant to the remaining corners in the same way. Blend the corners together with your finger. Again, don't try to make them perfect!

18 (BELOW) Once you've applied caulk around the perimeter of the tub, it's time to remove the tape. It needs to be removed before the caulk begins to set up. Starting in the corner, pull the tape straight off the wall. Try not to get any of the caulk residue from the tape on other surfaces.

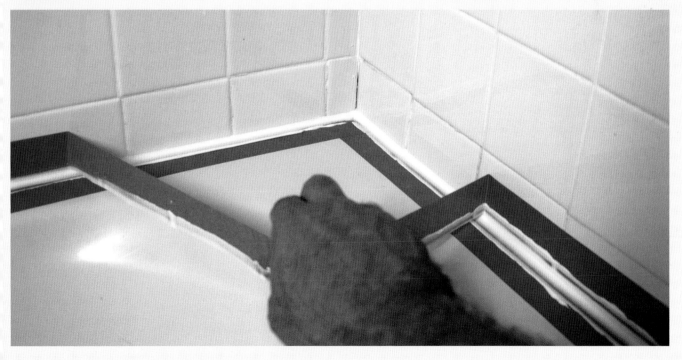

19 Remove the tape from the tub surface in the same manner. If it's easier to start from an outside corner, that's fine.

20 (LEFT) So far, so good. But have you been paying close attention to the detail? Did you notice the missing grout from the tiles in the corner? Give yourself 10 points if so. That, of course, needs to be filled or the caulk job is worthless — water will simply find its way into that crevice and begin its destructive journey down a different path. You don't necessarily need to use grout in that area — the caulk that we've been using in this project is fine (not to mention quicker and easier). If your grout is a different color, that changes things. Obviously, try to find a tub & tile caulk that matches.

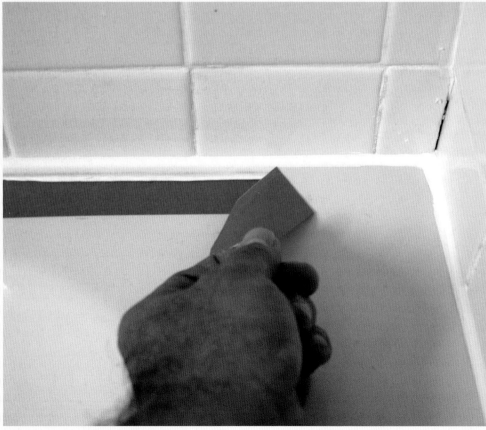

If you notice small areas of caulk that some-how found their way from the painter's tape to the fiberglass or porcelain, here's something you can try that's probably at arm's reach. Use a little toothpaste on an old rag to scrub off the dried caulk. Because the toothpaste has a polishing action, it can remove spots like this without damaging the finish underneath!

21 In either case, the fix is much like the rest of the job. I would suggest waiting at least 24 hours before fixing a situation like this. That will give the rest of the caulk already applied a chance to cure. Apply tape to both sides of the void and simply apply a bead of caulk in the same manner. Blend the new caulk line into the bead already created around the tub. Just another small insurance policy to keep the water routed correctly.

22 (PHOTOS AT LEFT) Allow the caulk to completely cure be-fore draining the tub and using the shower or bath! Check the caulk label for recom-mended cure times.

Life's Little Annoyances

Here are some tricks I learned over the course of the years while doing home improvement segments for various shows on HGTV and DIY. Some are short and sweet, others a little more time-consuming, but still effective.

They're all designed with one goal — to eliminate one of life's little annoyances.

CHAPTER 5

Stop Squeaky Floors

There is a castle in Japan known around the world for its squeaky floors. Built hundreds of years ago, the squeak in the floor is intentional — it would alert residents of any intruders. With that said, if you still want to make your home a little quieter, this is the project for you.

That little annoying squeak or creak you hear when you walk on certain areas of your flooring is actually (in most cases) the subflooring riding up and down on a loose nail. It's the friction between the nail and wood that causes the squeak.

In the picture at right you can see the layers that make up most floors. On top, the finished wood flooring (or other material), below that, the subflooring (often plywood, particle board or planks) and finally the floor joist (holding all of it up).

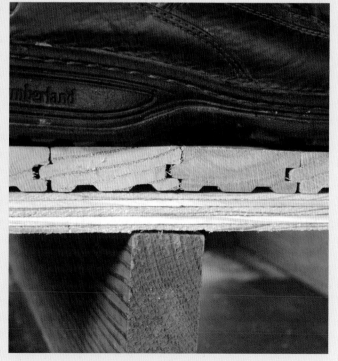

The nail holding the subflooring to the joist is visible above left. When someone stands on that area, the subflooring is compressed to the joist, causing the noise. That's our culprit, but unfortunately, the head of it is obscured by the finished floor (above right), so it's difficult to just "beat it back in"!

In some older homes, the noise may be coming from the floorboards themselves rubbing against each other. Over time, the wood in these old floors can shrink, leaving just enough space for movement and sound. If you think this could be your problem, here's a simple test and fix. Isolate the squeaky area and pour some talcum powder over the boards. Brush it into the cracks so it can act as a dry lubricant on the wood.

The Bracket Method

The first step always is to locate the problem area underneath the floor. You need access to the floor joists and subflooring. This might mean going into the basement, crawl space or garage.

Once you've located the squeaky area, take a look along the top of the ceiling joists. If you see a gap, that's the first place to start the fix. It helps to have a friend who can walk the floor above and apply pressure while you look for any movement of the subflooring. If the subflooring moves visibly up and down, the goal is to stop the movement.

① A view from below of the floor joists and the plank subflooring on top of them. Planks can be tricky and time-consuming when it comes to locating and stopping squeaks because you're dealing with numerous boards and more nails than you'd typically find in a sheet subflooring like plywood or OSB.

② This is a side view of the area where subflooring meets the floor joists. The gap between them should be eliminated if possible.

3 Attach a 1" L bracket — available for about $.25 at the hardware store — first to the subfloor using a 1" screw. Your subflooring should be ⅝" minimum and the finished flooring at least ½" on top of that. That totals just over an inch, so there shouldn't be a danger of driving the screw up through the finished flooring. To be sure, drive the screw slowly and have a friend watch for any evidence of it beginning to break the surface above. Use a shorter screw if necessary. Use a drill/driver to install the bracket. Keep it snug against the joist when installing it to the subfloor.

4 Next, weight needs to be applied to the floor above to close the gap as much as possible. Again, a helper comes in very handy in this situation. Once the gap has narrowed or closed, drive a second screw into the bracket, securing it to the floor joist. You should use a longer screw for the joist connection — 1½" long will be fine. This should be the end of the squeaks (at least in this area). You can move on to the next trouble spot!

The Shim Method

If you've located the problem area and don't have the option of compressing the floor above to eliminate the gap, here's a quick fix that can be temporary or permanent, giving you the option of using a different method later.

Use a wood shim — packages are available in the lumber or door and window department at the home improvement store — to immobilize the subflooring. Just slide the shim into the gap as far as it will go using hand pressure. Don't hammer it in or it could act as a wedge to worsen the gap! If you'd like to make this a permanent fix, just use some wood glue on the top and bottom of the shim to hold it in place.

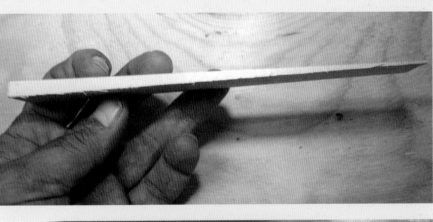

The Block Method

If you can't pinpoint the exact spot of the offending squeak, the block method may be a perfect solution. You need a short piece of 1×2 or 1×4. The length is determined by how long an area you want "cured." Usually, 12" to 24" is fine, but you could conceivably install blocking like this along the entire length of the joist, if that's what it takes.

You can save yourself a headache by pre-installing a couple of finish nails in the block before you put it in place. This way, you won't be juggling the board, the nails and the hammer.

Hold the block tightly against the subflooring in the area of the noise and drive the nails into the floor joist. You can add construction adhesive to create an even sturdier fix, but it's not mandatory.

A Trick for Carpeted Floors

If you have heavy pile carpet, here's another fix I learned from an old carpenter (they always have tricks up their sleeve!). This method actually closes the offending gap from above and minimizes subfloor movement. It won't work in all situations, but it may give you some inspiration.

Once the squeak is located, drive a 2" finish nail through the carpet's backing at an angle. By driving at a slight angle, it minimizes the chances of the nail loosening over time and creating another annoying noise!

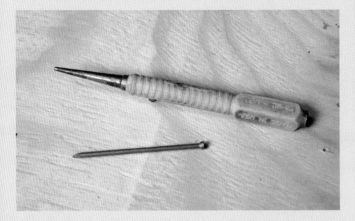

You'll need some finish nails and a nail set to try this.

Once the nail has been driven through the carpet and backing, there shouldn't be a visible hole on the surface.

This isn't my first or favorite method, but it can be handy to know in a pinch. The alternative to this method for carpeted floors with no access below is to peel the carpet back from the wall and make the fix, then re-stretch the carpet. Sounds like a lot of work....because it is.

You should also know that there are many packaged "fixes" on the store shelves. Be careful not to pay too much for a glorified bracket, when the first method here will do just about the same thing for a lot less.

On the other hand, I've seen some relatively sophisticated contraptions that sprang from the minds of clever people who most likely faced the same squeaky problem and developed a nice remedy. My first instinct is always to try the simplest path first...Murphy will attempt to make it complicated at some point during the project.

Use a nail set when the head is close to penetrating the backing. This will drive the nail completely through the backing and allow you to seat it correctly in the subflooring. Be sure to drive it in completely...you don't want to step on a protruding nail head later!

Repairing a Window Screen

OK, in the scheme of things, a hole or tear in a window screen is pretty low on the list of disasters. However, if the hole allows mosquitoes, flies and other annoying pests into your sanctuary, it may move up the list a few pegs.

Replacing an entire screen is relatively simple, for some screens, but not always possible on older homes. It's also time-consuming, and frustrating to get it stretched perfectly. So, while you contemplate the opening in your schedule to complete that task, here's a quick fix I learned years ago and presented on DIY. At least it'll save you a little on bug spray.

Holes and tears like this one can be caused by kids, animals, people — just about anything.

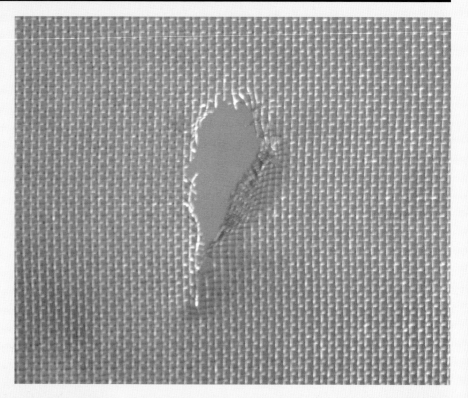

1 To create the repair, you'll need another piece of metal screen trimmed to a little larger than the damaged area. You'll see in a moment that the closer the size, the better the repair will look.

Use scissors or snips to cut off any excess. Pre-packaged patches like this are available at the hardware store if you don't have an old screen to cannibalize.

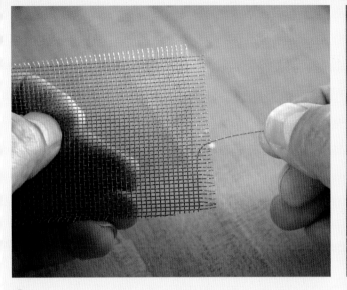

2 The next step requires some steady fingers. And be careful — the little wires that make up the screen are pretty sharp! Remove enough wires around the perimeter so that the cross-wires are protruding about ¼". When you're done, the patch should look like the one on the above right.

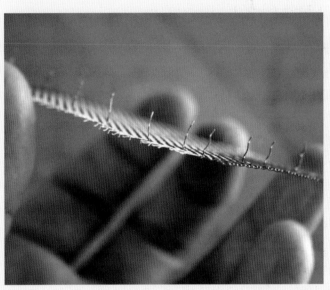

3 Next, bend one of these wires to a 90 degree angle about every ½" or so. Just be sure to get a couple close to each corner and several along each side. We'll be using these bent wires to attach the patch to the screen.

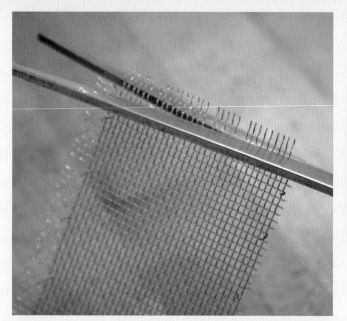

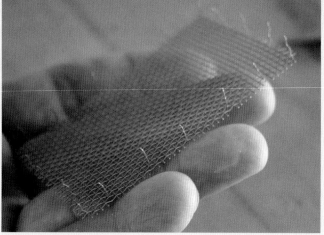

④ Trim off the remaining wires as close as possible to the edge of the patch so they'll be as inconspicuous as possible. The finished patch should look like the one above.

⑤ If you want the repair to look neat and tidy, you'll need to lay the screen over a scrap of wood. Then, use a marker and straightedge to draw a square or rectangle around the damaged area, as close as possible. Use a sharp razor knife (a new blade is a wise idea for a neater cut) to remove the damaged area of the screen. Be careful at the corners to prevent pulling the wires around the damage. Once the damage is cut out, we're ready to install the patch.

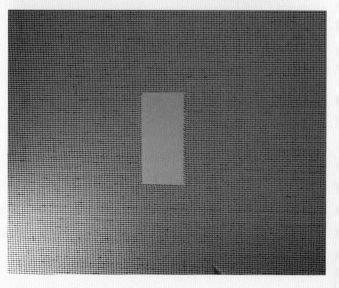

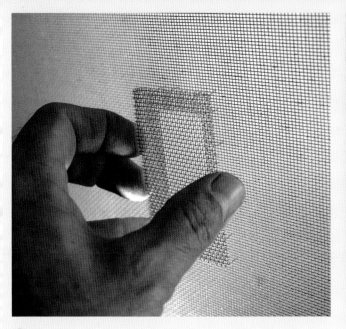

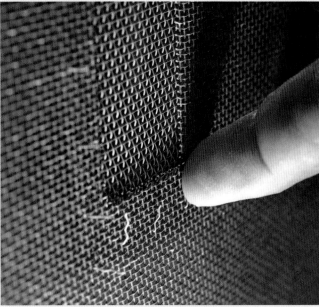

6 Place the patch against the hole. If you're satisfied with the size of the patch in terms of overlap, press the protruding wires through the screen around the hole.

7 Once the patch is flat against the existing screen, move to the other side and bend the attaching wires back over the screen. Be careful not to stick your finger. The problem is, it's nearly impossible to do this job with gloves. You get what I refer to as "fumble fingers."

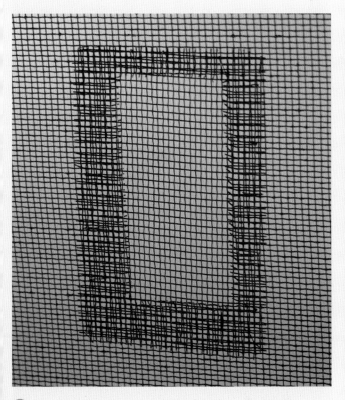

8 Once the wires are bent into place, take a look at the repair. If you're not satisfied with the way it looks (and, by the way, it'll never look perfect, so don't even go there), simply remove it and trim it back farther. Then reinstall. The patch on the left is a little large for my taste. The one on the right is just...right! If you decide to remove and repair the patch, just be careful that you don't break off any of the attaching wires. They can get rather brittle being bent back and forth.

Adjusting a Sticking Door

Sticking doors are another of life's little annoyances. I have a friend who simply stopped using an exterior door at her house because it sticks so badly. She nailed it shut. While that certainly eliminated the annoyance (she never fights with the door anymore), it created a new one...having to use a different door.

In most cases, a sticking door is simply caused by screws that have become loose or stripped. I remember my dad telling me to stop swinging on the door when I was a kid (come on, we've all done it!). Now I know why....he was in charge of door repairs at our house.

We're tackling an interior door in this project, but the fix can work for exterior doors as well.

A door is nothing more than a rectangular object placed into a rectangular opening and held there with hinges and a latch. Tolerances around a door are usually $^3/_{16}$" or less, so it doesn't take much movement out of square to start rubbing the door jamb.

Doors with three hinges are like seesaws turned on their side. The middle hinge is the seesaw pivot, in effect. That means that if the door is sticking on the upper right, there's likely a larger gap on the lower right and vice versa. Both of those gaps should be the same — and here's how you can get them back into alignment.

Tight & Bright

Clean, Tight & Bright — that was our motto in auto shop class in school. It was preached to us every day. I didn't fully appreciate its importance until I was older, of course. But if you make sure on any project that everything can be described that way, there's a good chance it will work and look good at the same time.

With that in mind, look at a sticking door in the same way. Make sure there are no foreign objects obstructing the hinge action (clean). Make sure all fasteners are doing their job (tight) and make sure that everything is generally polished (bright), in a manner of speaking. Keeping all the mechanisms bright and shiny goes a long way in keeping them in top operating shape!

1 The first and easiest thing to do is check the hinge pins. They can sometimes ride upward in the hinge due to lack of lubrication or dirt in the hinge barrel. If this happens, it can cause the door to sag slightly and rub on the latch side. To fix this issue, use a hammer with a piece of tape over the head to drive the hinge home. The tape helps minimize damage to the hinge finish or the paint in the door. Be gentle...it should only take a few short taps to seat the pin.

2 Once the hinge pins are sitting in the proper place, take a look at the hinge screws. They should all be present and accounted for — and screwed snugly in. Replace any missing screws and tighten any that may have come loose over time.

If you find that one of the screws simply turns without getting tighter, it's likely the hole has become stripped — it can no longer hold the screw tightly. The fix is simple. Remove the screw and insert a wood toothpick into the hole about an inch and snap it off. This will minimize the excess space in the hole and give the screw something to grab hold of. Replace the screw and tighten slowly to see if this helps.

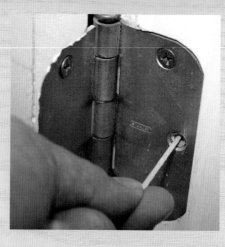

3 Next, look at the latch and strikeplate. Each will have a couple of screws that should be checked and tightened if loose. Screws that are as little as a fraction of an inch too proud of being seated properly can cause a door to stick. You'll generally see scratches made by the screws if this is the case. That would be a clue that they need tightening.

4 A high spot in the wood of the door can also cause it to stick. The sticking action will often leave a shiny, buffed mark where the friction is occurring. It could also just present itself as scratched paint. Although high spots could be present anywhere on the door's perimeter, they usually end up at the top and bottom corners. Look for the telltale missing paint or buffed spot, then use sandpaper wrapped around a small block of wood to smooth out the bump. The block keeps the paper flush against the side so that you don't round off the edges of the door. After every few strokes, test the door for proper operation.

My Goal

When I was growing up, our schools offered classes in both wood shop and automotive repair. I learned more in those classes from a common-sense standpoint than from the rest of my curriculum combined. Today, it seems video games and computers have become the new workshop and fewer of us are working — really working — with our hands. That scares me a lot.

My auto shop teacher, Mr. Frank Draves, constantly reminded students, "When you eat, you eat. When you sleep, you sleep. When you study, you study." His point was, live in the moment and focus fully on the task at hand. That's where inspiration lives. That's how creativity is nurtured.

I hope you've had the chance to tackle one or more of the projects on these pages. Hopefully, you discovered a way to improve your home and learned some new tricks along the way. If you found a new way to save energy or fix an expensive leak, you've made this book worth writing. Maybe you learned how to use a new tool or discovered a new way to use an old one; that means my goal has been met.

It was my intent for this book to be anything but just another home improvement guide. I wrote it to be more of an owner's manual for your home — the book you reach for when something breaks. I'd love for you to be inspired, even in some small way, to think outside the box. Don't simply throw away something when it gets broken; learn how to fix it.

Thanks for taking the time to read these words. Think about them. Pass the skills you learned to your children. Teach them to be self-reliant. It just may be the best gift you ever give them.

Books of Interest

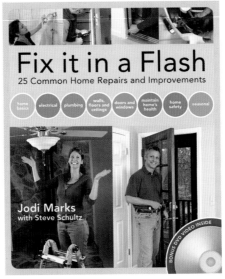

BACKYARD PROJECTS FOR TODAY'S HOMESTEAD

Convert your under-used yard into a veritable (and functional) oasis! Create your own rural homestead and improve your quality of life by building one or all of the 20 backyard projects in this book. Construction is easy, using the measured drawings and step-by-step photos. Also included is information on choosing durable materials, working with reclaimed lumber and applying finishes that hold up to the toughest outdoor conditions. From chairs and swings to chicken coops and pergolas, we've got a project for your backyard homestead.

Paperback, 160 pages.

FIX IT IN A FLASH

Authors Jodi Marks (a well-known home repair expert) and Steve Schultz know that doing all the fixes around a house should be a team effort, and that's how Jodi and Steve have approached home repairs. This book offers step-by-step photos for the 25 essential home repairs, and the bonus DVD gives you real-time information (and more helpful hints) on the most common of these. If you're feeling under-informed, (and slightly embarrassed to admit it) let Jodi and Steve take away your fears, and entertain you in the process with their couples approach to home fixes.

Paperback, 176 pages.

KITCHEN MAKEOVERS FOR ANY BUDGET

In *Kitchen Makeovers for Any Budget* author Chris Gleason offers his advice and how-to knowledge to help you make the correct decisions about whether to re-face or paint your present kitchen cabinets, add new appliances and cabinets, redo the workflow, move walls, etc. *Kitchen Makeovers for Any Budget* includes four complete remodeling projects; each one deals with a particular aspect of demolition, design and/or accessorizing. The companion DVD focuses on the design, workflow and accessories available to maximize your space and provide convenient storage solutions.

Paperback, 144 pages.

These books and other fine Betterway Home titles are available at your local bookstore and from online suppliers. Visit our website at www.betterwaybooks.com.